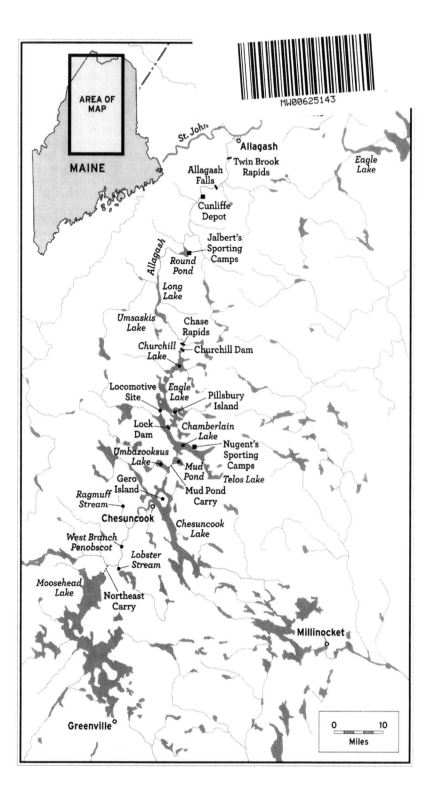

AREA OF MAP

MAINE

St. John

Allagash

Twin Brook Rapids

Allagash Falls

Eagle Lake

Cunliffe Depot

Jalbert's Sporting Camps

Allagash

Round Pond

Long Lake

Umsaskis Lake

Chase Rapids

Churchill Lake

Churchill Dam

Locomotive Site

Eagle Lake

Pillsbury Island

Lock Dam

Chamberlain Lake

Umbazooksus Lake

Nugent's Sporting Camps

Mud Pond

Telos Lake

Gero Island

Mud Pond Carry

Ragmuff Stream

Chesuncook

Chesuncook Lake

West Branch Penobscot

Lobster Stream

Moosehead Lake

Northeast Carry

Millinocket

Greenville

0   10
Miles

CANOEING MAINE'S
LEGENDARY ALLAGASH

Thoreau, Romance and Survival of the Wild

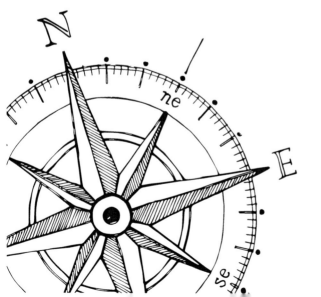

CANOEING MAINE'S
LEGENDARY ALLAGASH

Thoreau, Romance and Survival of the Wild

11/20/16

Susan,
Hope you enjoy
a wild ride by
canoe in Maine.
Best,
David

DAVID K. LEFF

HOMEBOUND
PUBLICATIONS
Independent Publisher of Contemplative Titles
STONINGTON, CONNECTICUT

HOMEBOUND PUBLICATIONS

Ensuring the mainstream isn't the only stream.

Visit us www.homeboundpublications.com

FIRST EDITION TRADE PAPERBACK

ISBN: 978-1-938846-33-5
Cover and Interior Designed by Leslie M. Browning
Cover Images by © Yarygin

Library of Congress Cataloging-in-Publication Data

Names: Leff, David K., author.
Title: Canoeing Maine's legendary Allagash: Thoreau, romance, and survival of the wild / David K. Leff.
Description: First edition. | Stonington, Conn. : Homebound Publications, 2016.
Identifiers: LCCN 2016028299 | ISBN 9781938846335 (pbk.)
Subjects: LCSH: Allagash River Valley (Me.)–Description and travel. | Canoes and canoeing–Maine–Allagash River. | Natural history–Maine–Allagash River Valley. | Leff, David K.–Travel–Maine–Allagash River Valley. | Thoreau, Henry David, 1817-1862–Travel--Maine.
Classification: LCC F27.A4 L44 2016 | DDC 974.1/25–dc23
LC record available at https://lccn.loc.gov/2016028299

10 9 8 7 6 5 4 3 2 1

1% GIVEN TO CHARITY

Homebound Publications greatly values the natural environment and invests in environmental conservation. Our books are printed on paper with chain of custody certification from the Forest Stewardship Council, Sustainable Forestry Initiative, and the Program for the Endorsement of Forest Certification. In addition, each year Homebound Publications donates 1% of our net profit to a humanitarian or ecological charity. To learn more about this year's charity visit www.homeboundpublications.com.

ALSO BY DAVID K. LEFF

The Last Undiscovered Place
Deep Travel
Hidden in Plain Sight
The Price of Water
Depth of Field
Tinker's Damn
Finding the Last Hungry Heart
Maple Sugaring

CONTENTS

PART I PUT IN

PART II WOODS & WATERS, 1983

PART III TAKE OUT

I sat there and forgot and forgot, until what remained was the river. On the river the heat mirages danced with each other and then they danced through each other and then they joined hands and danced around each other. Eventually the watcher joined the river, and there was only one of us. I believe it was the river.

—Norman Maclean, *A River Runs Through It*

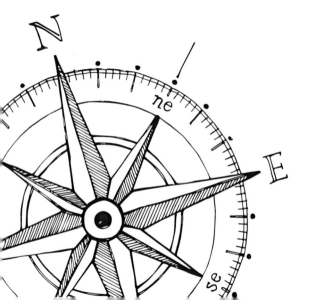

PART I

→

PUT-IN

The river is the ideal of continuity. It preserves the fluency of continual change and yet holds the one form. The river is so interesting because it offers a creative metaphor of the way the mind flows in and through experience.
—JOHN O' DONOHUE, *Eternal Echoes*

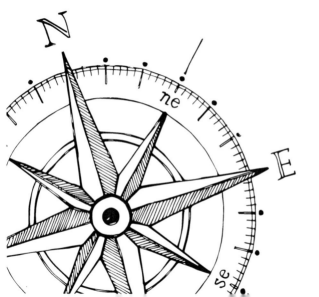

AN UNEXPECTED DISCOVERY

I magine you're a few months shy of turning sixty. Looking in a mirror, you find your twenty-something self staring back. Of course, it didn't happen precisely that way. I can't exactly say I saw my image reflected with the darker hair and smoother skin of youth. In a way I saw more. It was a deep, metaphorical mirror, almost a fairy-tale looking glass that not only illuminated a body more than thirty years younger, but drew me into the struggles and aspirations that created the person I am today. Yet this man was so remote in time and events that he felt more like a distant cousin.

I was no Benjamin Button falling back in time, nor had I stumbled upon Ponce de Leon's fountain. I was cleaning the attic in my home of three decades when I lifted a heavy box with a weak bottom. A flurry of papers dropped out, some landing in front of me and others floating down the narrow, uneven staircase. Cramped by the low ceiling, hot and sweating in August's unrelenting heat and humidity, I swore at the top of my lungs though no one was home to hear me. I grabbed a handful of the offending papers and began angrily shoving them into a black plastic trash bag. Suddenly I stopped. It was a manuscript. I began reading. I was transfixed.

Written in the mid 1980s, it was the narrative of a canoe trip I'd taken on northern Maine's legendary Allagash River a few years earlier. In the days before any of my work had seen print, I'd hoped to get the story published and sent it to a few outdoor journals without luck. Typed on an old Wang PC Classic I'd trashed long ago, the manuscript had no electronic copy. I'd put the document away, and like a misplaced safe-deposit box key, had quickly forgotten where I'd left it.

I carefully picked up the pages, brought them downstairs, and read all 31,000 words in one sitting at my kitchen counter, though I was tired and covered with dirt. It went down like a double shot of whiskey taken in one quick gulp. It certainly wasn't quite like Melville's granddaughter finding a tin breadbox containing *Billy Budd* in the long dead author's Pittsfield, Massachusetts home, but the print on the yellowed, dog-eared pages was remarkably engaging. It was not at all the stilted piece of juvenilia I expected when I first realized what I held.

Like a box of old family photographs, the manuscript ignited memories. Some I savored—triumphant rediscoveries of forgotten places and moments in the deep woods. Other fragments of this personal archaeology made me blush since it recounted an awkward and callow handling of a tangled and needlessly tumultuous relationship with my paddling partner who was also my lover. With the passage of time and forgetfulness, some of it purposeful, the recollections seemed remote, as if I were reading a letter from a long lost friend living in a distant land. It was me, but not who I am today. In some strange manner, I was looking at a prototype, an earlier and faultier version of my self.

I carefully filed the typescript away as a youthful artifact. I saved it in the same spirit that I kept grammar school drawings by my children years after they were no longer posted with refrigerator magnets. Too much time had passed, and changes on this well worn canoe route dated my experience. Furthermore, the story was personal, about the beginnings of a long term relationship that ended painfully and still seethed with irritable exasperation.

Friends soon convinced me that the story of my 1983 Allagash journey might be worth a read. First, they were right about the scarcity of other Allagash tales in that era starting, as I did, on the West Branch of the Penobscot River and then proceeding though the big headwater lakes down the Allagash to its confluence with the St. John River near the Canadian border. I called it the "classical route" because a West Branch start was commonly employed by nineteenth century sportsmen and rusticators before widespread development of logging roads offered other, more convenient canoe launch choices. At the same time, my trip differed from that of traditionalists because most of those who started on the West Branch paddled the big lakes without going down river. Later travelers who plied the river tended to start on the lakes and missed some characteristic Maine backwoods experiences offered by a West Branch beginning.

Not only had I paddled a somewhat different route than others, I apparently did so during in a kind golden interregnum in the river's wild character. Certainly, the Allagash of the early 1980s was a far cry from the wilderness Native Americans inhabited for centuries before Europeans appeared. But by the time I arrived, the river had healed somewhat from the worst of industrial logging that had prevailed in the forest from the mid nineteenth century to late in the twentieth. River log drives had recently ended and many current logging roads had yet to be built. It also antedated a spate of new motorized access points to the Allagash, and other infrastructure that started being built or rebuilt in the 1990s like parking lots, dams, boat ramps, and bridges. By 2002, such intrusive developments had led the non-profit watchdog group American Rivers to name the Allagash one of the most endangered watercourses in the nation.

Beyond its description of the river and woods, the manuscript was also a kind of personal time capsule. It laid bare my attitudes, delusions, and confidences about the world around me. In reading the story, I was most surprised at how little I listened to my own experience. Looking back over the decades, I realized that much of what I saw was what I wanted to see, both in the environment and in my connections with other people. Here was a revelation from the past that suddenly illuminated the present.

I was convinced by a couple fellow writers that in addition to interest in the journey, there might be some curiosity about my wrangle with a new relationship tested in the crucible of punishing physical effort in a remote place where neither party could just get up and walk away. This was not merely another backwoods canoe and camping story. It was direct testimony about a young person's effort to find meaning in adventure just beyond the comfort zone. It was an emotional tug-of-war featuring two youthful and strong-willed people pulling on opposite ends of experience under adverse circumstances requiring mutual dependence. Furthermore, unlike traditional memoirs, this was not a retrospective biographical sketch drawn from capricious memory, but an artifact of the past demanding reconciliation with the present. Regardless of what I thought now or the small myths I might have created to make it through my days, here was DNA evidence of what had actually happened.

THE THOREAU FACTOR

Maybe there is magic in a river flowing north, something that draws us the way the pole commands the compass needle. The Allagash is not a great river by traditional measures. Just over sixty miles long excluding the headwater lakes, it is but a tributary of the St. John. Though there is a roaring forty-foot waterfall, it flows through no great gorges and has rapids of little consequence. Despite grand claims, the region through which it passes is hardly a wilderness with its dams, campsites, roads, wrecked and rusting machinery and many other signs of humans past and present. At best, it is but a narrow backcountry gash in a commercial forest. Even its name, according to surveyor and mapmaker Moses Greenleaf's *A Survey of the State of Maine* (1829), is only a corruption for the Indian appellation of one of its principal water bodies—Allagaskwigamook, Bark Cabin Lake.

Regardless of such deficiencies, something continues to entice people to the Allagash as surely as the earliest native nomads were lured by the region's rich fish and game soon after retreat of glacial ice ten-thousand years ago. Like those ancients and their successors from time out of memory, many have come here during the few centuries of written history to earn a living—lumbermen, trappers, hunters, and farmers. But since the middle of the nineteenth century, individuals have also plied Allagash waters in a spirit of personal exploration, just to see what could be seen.

The name Allagash itself seems to exert a powerful, almost mystical influence over these riverine explorers, and even the uninitiated conjure romantic associations of feral adventure. Much of this magnetic fascination is owing to Henry David Thoreau.

I'd never have paddled the Allagash, and might not even have heard of the river were it not for Thoreau. It's a circumstance far from extraordinary. I'm just one among many that this pied piper of the wild has lured to Maine's backcountry. While the Concord, Massachusetts naturalist and transcendentalist didn't make the first, longest, or most extensive trip in this part of the world, he left the best written, inspiring, and most widely known accounts. In 1846, he and few others climbed Mount Katahdin, reaching the mountain via the Penobscot's West Branch and lakes in the Millinocket area, including Pemadumcook. Starting on Moosehead Lake in 1853 with a relative from Bangor and Penobscot Indian guide Joe Aitteon, he paddled as far as Chesuncook Lake. During 1857, he journeyed even further to the largest Allagash headwater lakes, Chamberlain and Eagle, accompanied by a hometown friend and Penobscot guide, Joe Polis.

Thoreau's poetic and muscular prose made the Maine woods come alive. His vivid descriptions and philosophical observations spiced with wry humor and arch social commentary put me among the dark, pointy spruces and windblown waters. Like an Old Testament prophet, he warned us to protect natural places as wellsprings of human inspiration and wonderment. Though he spent but a few weeks of his forty-four years in the Maine backcountry, it clearly touched his soul. His dying words—"moose" and "Indian"—harked back to his time on the Allagash. Under his tutelage, I learned that even a simple voyage could become an epic for those armed with a spirit of deep observation and a determination to probe beneath surfaces. He taught that destinations were less important than journeys.

I first glimpsed the Allagash region from Maine's highest point, Mount Katahdin's 5,267 foot summit. In the distance, the irregular lakes beckoned, sparkling east and north in what seemed an unbroken, trackless forest. Thoreau captured the sublimely majestic character of the region from the mountain's slopes as he, too, caught a first look at the Allagash country. "Talk of mysteries!" he wrote ecstatically. "Think of our life in nature,—daily to be shown matter, to come in contact with it,—rocks, trees, wind on our cheeks! the *solid* earth! The *actual* world! *the common* sense! *Contact! Contact! Who* are we? *Where* are we?" These seemed questions of the moment and for all times. I saw not just a rugged, wild topography, but a landscape of imagination. Going to the Allagash would be a kind of pilgrimage in the great man's paddle strokes and footsteps.

Thoreau's words may have infiltrated my Allagash dreams, but a confluence of factors drew me there, and it now almost seems I hardly had a choice. To start, I'd spent almost a decade as an Appalachian Mountain Club volunteer opposing the Dickey-Lincoln hydroelectric dam. Slated to flood the river's confluence with the St. John, it would have destroyed fifty-seven miles of free-flowing river and about 100,000 acres of woodland while doing incalculable damage to native fish and wildlife from brook trout to deer. During that time, I developed an even more ardent interest in natural areas, rivers, and forests after taking an environmental policy job with the Connecticut state legislature. Furthermore, under the spell of Thoreau, I harbored ambitions of writing backwoods travel essays both picturesque and practical. All this conspired to stir a puny young man with poor hand-eye coordination, always the last picked for any ballgame, to engage in a singular opportunity to prove his athleticism.

In true Thoreauvian style, I devoured every map, book, and article I could find about the region. I discovered a host of nineteenth and twentieth century adventurers, sportsmen, and other visitors who had floated Allagash waters and been inspired to put pen to paper. Though it seemed to gainsay a wild image, no other river had inspired so many stories of remote adventure. Before ever wetting a paddle, I traveled the Allagash many times in print.

Rather than dissuade me from writing about what might have been the best documented wild area in the country, I was determined to take these fellow travelers with me, to explore in time as well as space by comparing what my predecessors saw with what I would find. What truth, I wondered, remained in the potency of the name "Allagash?" I would discover not only a place for communion with nature and a test of my physical stamina and outdoor skills, but connections with generations of kindred human beings.

Regardless of whether they mentioned him, all these diarists of adventure seemed a footnote to Thoreau. Among them were Theodore Winthrop, whose Life in the Open Air, about an 1856 trip with famed Hudson River School painter Frederic Church, was published posthumously in 1863. A lawyer, writer, and world traveler, he was a direct descendent of a Connecticut colonial governor and one of the first Union officers killed in the Civil War. Another was Hartford, Connecticut writer, photographer, and artist Thomas Sedgwick Steele who lavishly illustrated his books. Within the elegant marble rectangle of Yale's Beinecke Library, I eagerly read his Paddle and Portage: From Moosehead Lake to the Aroostook River, published in 1882, and later Canoe and Camera: A Two Hundred Mile Tour Through the Maine Forests (1880). Boston lawyer Lucius Hubbard, who would become Michigan's state geologist, wrote a guidebook and map to the Moosehead Lake region. In 1884, he recounted some of his backcountry trips in Woods and Lakes of Maine, a volume whose direct prose and attention to detail has well withstood the test of time. Fisherman and hunter Gerrit Smith Stanton, son of abolitionist Henry B. Stanton and suffragette and feminist Elizabeth Cady Stanton, wrote of his Maine woods travels in Where the Sportsman Loves to Linger: The Allagash, the East and West Branches of the Penobscot, published in 1905. U. S. Chief Justice Melville Fuller found the book "most excellent and vivid." Maine historian Fannie Hardy Eckstorm, an expert on Penobscot Indians who knew both of Thoreau's native guides, wrote in her journals about West Branch paddles with her father late in the nineteenth century.

Coincident with the apex of wide scale lumbering, Maine woods literature becomes relatively sparse until late in the twentieth century. In 1961, U.S. Supreme Court Justice William O. Douglas published an Allagash chapter in his book *My Wilderness: East to Katahdin*, and called for the river's permanent protection. Little more than a decade later, novelist and essayist Edward Hoagland's article "Fred King on the Allagash" (1973) appeared in *Audience*, and in 1975 Pulitzer Prize winning author John McPhee's trip with canoe builder Henri Vaillancourt was published as The Survival of the Bark Canoe after first seeing print in *The New Yorker*. History professor J. Parker Huber, a leader of Thoreauvian trips to Maine, published *The Wildest Country: A Guide to Thoreau's Maine* in 1981.

Each author brought something different to the Allagash. Among some early writers, I found not only a love of outdoor adventure and the natural world, but desires to promote tourism, a macho roughing-it image, and boasting about how many fish and other animals they could kill. Later accounts often advocated river and wildlife conservation, along with a determination to discover what wilderness remained on the fabled river. Regardless of their viewpoint, each page whet my appetite. My own Allagash experience would become enlarged by worlds gone by. I saw not only with my own eyes, but through those who had come before me.

Canoeing the region was to be more than a long camping trip by water. It was a vision quest that would not only test my skills as an outdoorsman and a writer, but the reality of the world I'd dreamed of through books. I'd found a literary cartography joined to personal geography.

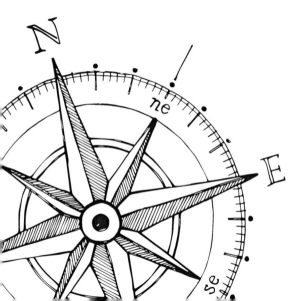

RIVER REBORN

I was a young man in my twenties when I paddled the Allagash, but in a way the much storied river was even younger. It had been reborn in 1966 as the "Allagash Wilderness Waterway" by act of the Maine state legislature which sought "to develop the maximum wilderness character" of a 92 mile-long corridor of lakes and rivers from Telos Lake in the south to West Twin Brook in the north, about five miles upstream of Allagash Village at the confluence of the St. John. Later that year, Maine citizens passed a $1.5 million bond issue for the area's protection, an amount matched a few months after by the federal government.

In 1970, the Allagash was designated "wild" under the National Wild and Scenic Rivers Act, and became the first federally protected river administered by a state. Although "wild" rivers are usually free flowing and have limited road access, an exception was made for historic reasons despite dams and some roads. It was a time of bitter controversy about the region when some called for a national recreation area or national park, and others favored new hydroelectric dams and resisted any regulation of powerful timber interests. The final result was viewed as a compromise.

Conservation of the Allagash region is an idea Thoreau envisioned more than a century earlier, concluding his "Chesuncook"

essay with a like suggestion. "[Why should we not] have our national preserves . . . in which the bear and panther, and some even
of the hunter race, may still exist, and not be 'civilized off the face
of the earth,' . . . not for idle sport or food, but for inspiration and
our own true recreation?" A prescient notion, it would still be more
than a decade before the nation's first national park was designated
far to the west.

The bureaucratic reality of the "protected" Allagash is that land
400 to 800 feet from the water is owned by the State of Maine.
In this zone, non-recreational activity is severely limited and new
seasonal camps, timber harvesting, and construction are prohib-
ited. A restricted area within a mile of high water requires forestry
and other activities on private land to be conducted in accordance
with state approved management plans. It sounds like a reasonable
policy, but the reality is not so reassuring.

The Dickey-Lincoln Dam that worried me in the 1970s has
long been consigned to the dustbin of failed pork barrel projects.
But dam projects have not disappeared. In the 1990s, the state replaced the traditional timber crib Churchill Dam at the head of
the river with an industrial steel and concrete structure out of scale
with the waterway and historically inappropriate. The work was
done illegally without necessary federal permits. Maintenance of
other dams or their possible replacement lurks in the future and
may adversely affect the river's wild character if not carefully con-
ceived and executed.

Less grand, more insidious threats because of their smaller,
less noticed scale and subtle cumulative impacts continue to
erode wildness. Long dormant logging roads have been reopened.
Wealthy and sometimes politically connected individuals building
private camps and second homes on enormous nearby tracts, so
called "kingdom lots," often push for their own snowmobile trails,
canoe harbors other access that perforates protected lands. Over
the years, legislative efforts to deauthorize the waterway, cut funds,

make the supervisor's position a political appointment, and other threats have sometimes compromised legal protections.

With the occasional sounds and sights of timber harvesting beyond a beauty screen of trees, the Allagash remains a bit short of dictionary definitions of "wilderness" and "wild." In reality, the terms are more aspirational than actual, goals that are sometimes corrupted in practice. Still, the name Allagash remains synonymous with untamed nature. It is a land of contradictions and juxtapositions. In 1983, it seemed the perfect place for me to test my mettle.

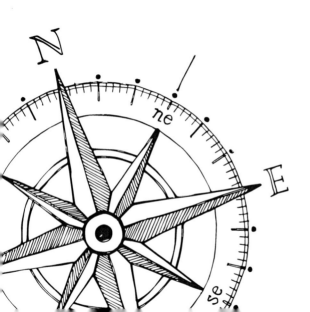

ECOLOGY OF PARTNERSHIP

eeding someone to share my Allagash journey, I chose the woman I'd been dating for little more than a year. We'd been living together for a few months and she seemed eager. Furthermore, I knew that if I'd chosen another companion, resentments difficult to overcome would have surfaced. While I had some more experienced and stronger potential colleagues in mind, the dynamics of relationships left me no real choice. In a short time, I'd become deeply invested in our connection and I dearly wanted it to work.

I'll give her the pseudonym Alice and change a few indentifying particulars so as to help reduce the possibility of any misunderstanding at my characterizations. It was the first name that occurred to me. Maybe I used it because among female names it stands near the head of the alphabet. More likely, there are deeper psychological reasons. As a child, I'd read and reread Lewis Carroll. Being with this woman, I found myself, like Carroll's Alice, falling down the deep well of a rabbit hole and into a strange and unfamiliar land where inner and outer experiences were distorted and entangled.

We'd met at an Adirondack Mountain Club lodge in New York over dinner. It was a long table where food was served family style and conversation passed around as easily as trays of beef and bowls of potatoes and broccoli. I was an experienced backpacker and hiker who had just finished climbing all sixty-something of the 4,000 foot peaks in New England. She was an ingénue on the rock strewn and rooty trails of the region, out to try something new and test herself. We were both refugees from long-term relationships that had ended recently, a case of reciprocal rebound.

Each of us was searching for something beyond a new summit to conquer and we quickly fell into conversation and, later that evening, into much more in the carpeted bed of my red Chevy Luv pickup truck. Despite living at some distance from one another, the relationship blossomed suddenly and beyond expectations. Though our rapid fusion appeared too fast for some friends, it felt natural and almost inescapable, like the gravity driven momentum of extra large and fast steps one takes descending a mountainside.

We laughed at how different we were. She was from a family that traced itself back to the Mayflower while I was a third generation American with grand-relatives who had fled a pogrom in Eastern Europe. Her father and previous generations had graduated from Yale while my dad was a high school dropout. Her family was full of discreet Yankees while my relatives were mostly boisterous New Yorkers. My parents divorced when I was a boy, hers were together until death parted them. She went to an elite woman's college while I attended a large state university. She studied science. I reveled in the humanities.

We found comfort in the old saying that opposites attract, like magnets. Nevertheless, we learned that relationships were more a matter of chemistry than physics. We each discovered something intoxicating when mixed together that we lacked alone. But ultimately, neither physics nor chemistry was as important as the complex biology of two independent and interdependent organisms living and growing in that seventeen-foot Petrie dish of emotions called a canoe.

Of course, the trip meant something much larger and more expansive to me than could possibly have occurred to her. I had a significant personal agenda to achieve, and she might not have come along had she been clearly aware of it. No doubt some of the emotional shoals and rapids that hindered our progress were caused by the urgency of my expectations.

Alice confided that paddling the Allagash was a one-of-a-kind opportunity for her. She was almost tipsy with excitement for an experience so far beyond previous exploits. As she saw it, I was her ticket to something fascinating and possibly life changing. Beyond that, Alice never fully revealed her motivations, so I could never completely fathom whether the voyage was successful in her eyes. It was simply never anything we talked about, though in retrospect it seems as much a necessity for a good trip as paddles or bug dope.

To Alice, this might have seemed no more than a particularly high-end canoe-camping adventure, but to me it was a rite of passage, an initiation. I was too committed to let it fail or fall short in any way. As a result, I probably ignored some obvious relationship warning signs because they would have disrupted the trip. I thus must take a goodly share of responsibility for friction on the voyage, and for what would happen next. I knew I was testing myself against wind, black flies, rough water, rain, and exhausting portages. But as a backpacker who had traveled woodland paths alone for weeks at a time, I didn't fully realize that in a canoe I'd be testing myself against the temperament of another person. What was truly most important only emerged later as I discovered that human confluences were much less discernable, smooth, and logical than those of rivers. My time on the Allagash was a watershed.

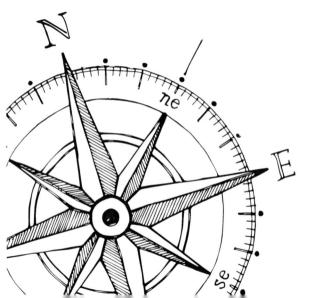

PART II

→

WOODS & WATERS

1983

Let us probe the silent places, let us seek what luck betide us;
Let us journey to a lonely land I know.
There's a whisper on the night-wind, there's a star agleam to guide us,
And the Wild is calling, calling . . . let us go.
—Robert W. Service, *The Call of the Wild*

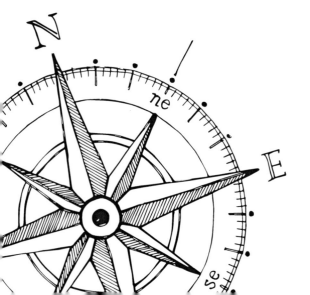

CLASSICAL BEGINNING

A lice and I began our voyage in the bright, early morning sunshine of September 5, 1983. We drove north on the road paralleling the east shore of forty-mile-long Moosehead Lake, having spent the night at an inn in Greenville, a tight little village situated at the lake's south end. Water beckoned from the window of our second-floor room in the elegant Victorian structure, sparkling along the uneven treed shoreline with hilly terrain beyond.

After traveling along most of the lakeshore, pavement yielded to hard-packed earth rutted from erosion and heavy use. We passed through a paper company checkpoint after satisfying a guard's curiosity. Pebbles pinged against the car frame and we kicked up clouds of dust. With the added windage of a canoe, perched like an ungainly bicorne hat on my Datsun's roof, the vehicle shook like an amusement park ride. Although travel was slow on the teeth-rattling road, it was still only a couple hours before we were alongside the West Branch of the Penobscot River at the northern terminus of a portage from Moosehead Lake called Northeast Carry. It wasn't always so easy to get there.

Before the advent of roads, the usual route was to take a steamer from Greenville the length of Moosehead Lake to Northeast Cove

at the carry's south end, though on his 1857 trip Thoreau canoed
there. Travelers have often remarked on how little the elevation
changes between lake and river. Nevertheless, the two-mile trip
crosses the divide between the Kennebec and Penobscot watersheds.

With four-wheel-drive vehicles that now negotiate many rough
logging roads threading through the woods and float planes that
easily land on the remotest lakes, destinations on a Maine woods
trip grow increasingly less meaningful than how to get there. How
you begin sets a tone. It highlights the philosophy of the journey
and its degree of physical effort. I worried that Alice and I had lost
something valuable by not traveling on Moosehead and portag-
ing Northeast Carry, a trip I'd lived vicariously many times in the
words of long gone writers. I glanced down the rutted, dirt paved
corridor longingly, freeing my imagination to roam the wide path
between the trees.

Though it's been an Indian artery of travel for centuries,
Northeast Carry was not always in the best shape. Despite earlier improvements to the narrow footpath, the 1837 expedition of
Maine's first state geologist, Charles T. Jackson, found the way "out
of repair, muddy, and encumbered by fallen trees and bushes."

Only after 1847, when the state granted a charter to the
Moosehead Lake Railway Company, was there substantial improvement. For the ease of the traveling public, a log railroad was
constructed on which a cart was drawn by an ox. New York based
adventurer Theodore Winthrop, traveling a few years before the
Civil War with painter friend Frederic Church, best described a
trip aboard this labor saving conveyance.

> Our cloven hoofed engine did not whirr turbulently along,
> like a thing of wheels. Slow and sure must the knock-
> kneed chewer of cuds step from log to log. Creakingly the
> train followed him, pausing and starting and pausing again
> with groans of inertia. A very fat ox was this, protesting

every moment against his employment, where speed, his duty, and sloth, his nature, kept him bewildered by their rival injunctions. Whenever the engine driver stopped to pick a huckleberry, the train, self breaking, stopped also, and the engine took in fuel from the tall grass that grew between the sleepers.

The passage took Winthrop an hour which, although slower than a man can walk the distance even loaded with gear, nevertheless saved wear and tear on the body and required only a single trip. Thoreau used the ox railroad in 1853, but carried by hand with his guide in 1857. In any event, the useful life of such conveyances is apparently not great. A quarter century later, only a few charred and decaying timbers testified to its existence alongside the wagon road that then hauled people and gear to the West Branch.

Horse and wagon were undoubtedly a vast advance and cost $1.50 for gear and canoe. Like all modern means of transportation, it was subject to technical difficulties. Artist and author Thomas Sedgwick Steele of Hartford, who passed this way in the 1880s, found himself halfway over the carry when the horses suddenly stopped, absolutely refusing to budge. The driver had run out of oats! No amount of coaxing or cajoling would get the animals moving. It was only after considerable thought on the matter and much frustration that they arrived at a solution. With the guides pushing with all they had from behind and Steele holding the empty oat bag in front of the horses, they made spasmodic progress. A dusty, unpaved, but relatively broad road, passable by cars, now does service between Moosehead and the West Branch, though I was told it is seldom used.

Until well into the twentieth century, the West Branch was the traditional entrance to the Allagash. Put-ins at Telos and Chamberlain Lakes further north and east are far more common today, because they are on the state-owned portion of the route and easily accessible by motor vehicle. But in the days before roads crisscrossed Maine's dense forests, this river was not only a conduit for logs on their way to sawmills, it was a traveler's highway into the woods. I might not have crossed Northeast Carry from Moosehead, but I was determined to make a traditional West Branch start.

Of course, not many Allagash travelers start here anymore even though paper company roads enable cars to go around the lake directly to the river and avoid the drudgery of the carry. But, bucking the trend like Alice and me, that's just what urbane essayist John McPhee did on his trip with quirky birch bark canoe maker Henri Vaillancourt in the 1970s. The two were using that classical Indian-style vessel made of tree bark stitched together with spruce roots. Employing the right boat, they needed to begin in the right place. Naturally, they chose the classical river start to an Allagash adventure, used for generations, twice by Henry David Thoreau.

WEST BRANCH

The river was wide and silent, bouncing sunlight from its taut surface like a trampoline. We were fidgety from the jarring logging-road ride. But the river exerted a soothing influence, drew out my imagination and placed me far into the evergreen woods, a realm alive with fresh sights, sounds, and smells.

As I stood mesmerized by the river, I felt the slight pulse of a headache. The sun was bright and we were hot and dry. Everything inside the car and trunk was covered with a fine layer of khaki-colored road dust, a condition that we had optimistically thought was limited to the vehicle's outside. Unloading the car and organizing the gear, my initial euphoria at having reached what I thought would be the raw edge of wilderness slowly diminished. Imagination collided with topographic reality.

As I expected, there were a few other cars parked here and, thankfully, just enough space for our own. But these were not the only signs of civilization. Directly across the river was a log cabin, and just downstream was a compound of small buildings. After all the deep woods visions we had carried and talked about for months, Alice and I suddenly felt the metallic taste of disappointment at these impositions on our notions of wilderness.

My chagrin faded when I remembered that civilized intrusions were not a recent phenomenon. In fact, the situation seemed to have improved in the last 130 or so years. In the 1850s, Thoreau found a sixty-acre clearing with a log camp and a home.

Historian Fannie Hardy Eckstorm, who as a young woman passed this way in 1889 with her father and a guide, enjoyed room and board at Luce's. She described a barroom "papered now with gilded paper, the woodwork . . . stained in cherry" with a curving bar behind which was "a triangular cupboard." The "front room," she noted, "has a piano and some chairs," which she termed fashionable, as well as pictures on the wall that "are scriptural and patriotic." They spent the evening in the parlor "entertained most of the time by Mrs. Luce, who after all did little more than to listen and make aimless remarks."

Grateful that we had no Mrs. Luce to heed, I stood quietly staring into the water, marveling how all the activity once here had wound down to the sluggish pace of the river. Next thing I knew, Alice grasped my shoulder, signaling she was ready to lift the boat from the car and pack our gear between the thwarts.

Alice is a freckle-faced dynamo of energy, a willful, hazel-eyed woman with long, curly, ginger hair and a warm gap-tooth smile. We'd recently committed to a "serious relationship," an exclusive franchise on each other's affections to see where it would lead. Following a couple instructional whitewater lessons and a few short day trips, we opted for the quiet and fresh air of a canoeing vacation. In the excitement of planning and the newness of travel, we had not fully contemplated how our young and still fragile relationship might fare in the pressured close quarters of a week-and-a-half of paddling. We knew our athletic skills and outdoor knowledge would be tested, not expecting that diplomacy and a thick skin would prove more valuable assets.

After loading the boat, we stood on the bank a few moments just staring, taking a mental snapshot for our memories. Stuffed with colorful baggage, the vessel was filled like a skycap's cart at the airport. Most of the gear was stored in a bright red and a green backpack attached to which were bulging, blue stuff sacks with sleeping bags and a rolled mat. An orange daypack contained food and cookware, and a small granite-colored pack was filled with fishing lures, monofilament line, reels, and a couple collapsible rods. Brilliant yellow life vests topped the whole collection which was tied down with nylon rope. It was, hopefully, everything we would need for at least a dozen days in the woods.

We must have spent forty hours buying, organizing, and packing our gear. All the food from granola to crackers to cheese had to be repackaged and triple wrapped in resealable plastic bags. The same was true for maps, toilet paper, matches, extra batteries, the rudimentary medical kit, and many other necessities of comfort and safety. Sleeping bags and clothing were also triple wrapped, but in large black plastic garbage bags. My Optimus 8-R backpacking stove, World War II era mess kit, trout knife, canteen, and the like were left unprotected since they could get wet with little or no harm.

The only items quadruple wrapped were my notebooks, pens, and pencils. I considered them my most valuable cargo. Without these writers' tools the trip would too quickly fade in memory and my ability to write an account of the voyage would evaporate. Without writing, the trip wouldn't feel completely real.

It was a tedious process of sorting, arranging, categorizing and figuring what would fit in what pouch or pocket of what pack. After all, we had to ensure we had enough food and supplies and the right equipment since there was no hope of procuring anything more. We poured over maps, made estimates of our likely progress and accounted for rainy and windbound days. Being a new couple, it was exhilarating to plan a miniature life together.

Naturally, we had disagreements over what to take. Every meal had to include foods we would both eat. Clothing took up a lot of space and had to be minimal. Luxuries like an extra pair of boots and the size of books for reading in inclement weather had to be carefully considered. We argued over a lantern because it was bulky and needed fuel. As a long-time backpacker, I was delighted that, despite a few portages, weight would not be an issue. As someone used to cramming everything into a single pack, the amount of stuff we took seemed positively opulent. Alice, however, saw asceticism in our equipage, if not downright privation.

Our sixteen-foot-long, seventy-eight pound green canoe was of Vermont manufacture and made of Royalex, a plastic laminate. A traditional cigar-shaped vessel, it was not unlike an Indian birch bark in its compromise between strength and lightness. Unlike that ancient material however, Royalex is almost indestructible. If Royalex had grown on trees in the Maine woods beside white birch, I'm sure Native Americans, being very practical, would have chosen the former. The boat had a low rise at bow and stern to reduce interference by wind, and a V-shaped hull rather than a keel, a compromise to ease navigation on lakes while avoiding getting caught on rocks in river rapids. Ash gunwales and thwarts along with cane seats gave the modern material a traditional look reminiscent of early twentieth century wood and canvas canoes.

Thoreau's first guide, Joe Aitteon, had a birch nineteen-and-a-half feet long and painted green, which he thought weakened the pitch used to seal seams and made it leak. Four years later, Thoreau measured the canoe Joe Polis had recently built at eighteen-and-a-quarter feet long, estimating that it weighed "not far from eighty pounds." Neither vessel had seats, though cedar splints were provided against the thwarts on which to lean a tired back while sitting on the boat's bottom. Thoreau and his companion "paddled by turns in the bows, now sitting with our legs extended, now sitting upon our legs, and now rising upon our knees," but he found none of the positions comfortable and eventually sat on the thwarts or stood up.

"The most beautifully simple of all vehicles," McPhee pronounced the canoe. With a hull "modeled on the thoracic structure of vertebrates," it is evidence "of the genius of humankind." Although materials innovations have been tested in canoes for well over a hundred years, the basic design has never been improved. Whether wood and canvas, fiberglass, aluminum, or plastic laminate like ours, the fundamental architecture remains the same.

I marveled at how McPhee could, in a couple phrases, find the very essence of the canoe and its connection to humanity regardless of the materials used to construct it. Angular and erudite, this long time *New Yorker* essayist and teacher of writing at Princeton was equally deft at describing a Manhattan art museum and the Alaskan wilds. I wanted not only to follow his Thoreauvian canoe route, but his knack for essays as lively as fiction. He knew the rhythm and flavor of words and could capture the quintessence of a person or place with breathtaking brevity. By seeing what he saw, perhaps I could learn how to make language flow from experience with the same crystalline perfection.

Mosquitoes had begun buzzing around us, so we slathered on some Ole Time Woodsman bug dope we'd procured on a last minute, two a.m. excursion to L.L. Bean a couple days earlier. In fierce sunshine, we shoved our canoe into the dark, placid West Branch. The river was quiet and deep, and when we stopped paddling a moment, movement was hardly perceptible. Nevertheless, the current's power was visible in the way in which it snatched a stray leaf or bowed a stick stuck upright in muddy shallows.

Banks were often high, evidence of the river's more powerful and energetic spring character. But on this September day, the water flowed deliberate and measured. At times it was a corridor steeply walled with a palisade of evergreens, the place I had conjured in imagination after reading Thoreau's description of "a narrow canal through an endless forest." But there were frequent meadows with elegantly sculpted elms arching toward the sky. Cedar, larch, and birch were common.

I found the river remarkably the same as fellow travelers had described it for over 130 years. There seemed a communal outlook and I felt camaraderie with those who had gone before, a common experience shared over time, a bond among writer-adventurers and this timelessly intriguing place.

The West Branch just below Northeast Carry is a sluggish, glassy surfaced stream. Perhaps influenced by artistic genius companion Frederic Church, Winthrop evokes a painterly image, finding "a current, unrippingly smooth, but dimpled ever with the whirls that mark an underflow deep and shady. No northern forest, rude and gloomy with pines, stood stiffly and unsympathizingly watching the graceful water, but cheerful groves and delicate coppices opened in vistas where level sunlight streamed."

About my age when he canoed here, Winthrop was a Byronic character with thick, dark hair and a bushy beard. After graduating Yale, he had traveled through Europe during the revolutions of 1848. Later he rode to California on horseback, traversed the Oregon Trail, paddled across Puget Sound in a dugout canoe, and surveyed a canal route in Panama. I envied his audacity, and the fact that he found the slow moving West Branch worthy of his time buoyed my sense of adventure.

With the strong, quiet water carrying him, Winthrop thought it "needless and impertinent to toil." In the warm lazy sunshine, Alice and I also rested our paddles and watched the shore slowly pass. We were hitchhikers on the current, hobos riding a freight. With no pressure or needed effort, we paddled at will. The canoe split great billowing cloud reflections on the water.

We relaxed and marveled to each other on the storybook beauty. The affection between us seemed almost palpable, fortified by the balmy air and tranquil river, revealed in the soft green forest against an azure sky.

Two-and-a-half miles below Northeast Carry, Lobster Stream flows in or out of the West Branch depending on water level. It enters at a low, marshy area. A small wooden bridge crosses just above its mouth. One party of nineteenth century travelers startled a caribou nearby and regretted they were not quicker with a gun. Another group frightened a deer just before reaching here, and saw signs of beaver activity. Our glimpse of wildlife here was not so fortunate.

Passing the confluence, we heard the gargling din of an outboard motor and spied a beat-up aluminum canoe reflecting battleship gray in the water. A well curved woman occupied the bow like a figurehead, and a man wearing a red-check flannel shirt sat in the stern, his hand on the motor. As we passed, we saw a third passenger lying prostrate amidships—a black bear with thick glistening fur, its tan facemask framing a powerful snout. A rifle lay atop the limp animal.

The current increases so subtly after Lobster Stream that it seems hardly worth a comment. Oddly enough, Thoreau and other paddlers have been moved to write about it. Maybe they were so bored with the sluggish river that the slightest acceleration caused excitement. On a thoroughfare such as this, without the signs and placards typically found on roads, it may be that we develop a more intuitive notion of landmarks, be they the current, trees, or banks. For safety and welfare, backcountry travelers must of necessity notice changes in the environment regardless of whether they are obvious or momentous. Maybe it's this intensive way of looking that invites us to focus on wildlife along this quiet reach.

We heard many kingfishers screeching as they took kamikaze dives at the water. Long-legged great blue herons were poised like ballet dancers. Gray Canada jays performed antics in the trees, and a council of chickadees echoed from the forest's edge. The alluring, longing, and quavering whistles of white-throated sparrows seemed to call us further into the woods, like the sirens that sung to Odysseus. We, however, did not cover our ears, but let ourselves be drawn ever deeper into the heart of the forest. Thoreau found the white-throated the prevailing bird of northern Maine, "a very inspiriting but almost wiry sound." He also saw orange flashes of redstart wings flitting through the dense greenery. Eckstorm noted black ducks, osprey, nuthatches and Canada jays, which she called "meatbirds." Illustrating a significant attitude adjustment from then to now, her father reflexively shot at and wounded a hawk flying across the river.

We passed six cow moose, including one with a calf, that first afternoon—the most we would see in a single day. Apparently, moose have always been quite abundant on the West Branch. The 1837 geological team commonly saw their tracks in the mud, and in the 1970s McPhee encountered many "great cloven depressions." Thoreau's 1853 companion, George Thatcher, shot one of the big animals near the mouth of Pine Stream. Following a trail of disturbed vegetation and occasional blood along the narrow tributary, Aitteon tracked it down and found the still warm carcass in rocky shallows about three-and-a-half miles upstream.

Thoreau had a true desire for knowledge about Indian ways, but was sometimes ambivalent about the reality. When Attien skinned the moose with a pocket knife, Thoreau found it a "tragical business" and was taken aback by the "ghastly naked red carcass." Later, however, he enjoyed the fried meat for supper, finding "it tasted like tender beef with perhaps more flavor; sometimes like veal."

Looking like ungainly, slightly humpbacked horses on stilt legs, most of the moose we saw were wading in the shallows, feeding on plants which they pulled up with great splashes of water draining from their muzzles. Standing six feet tall at the shoulders, with large pendulous snouts, they seemed elegant and beautiful despite their awkward and powerful appearance. Their dark sad eyes and soft brown fur evoked Teddy bear reminiscences. Though Thoreau found the animals "singularly grotesque and awkward to look at," they nevertheless made him think of "great frightened rabbits, with their long ears and half inquisitive half frightened looks." Despite their size and obvious strength, these creatures were quiet and gentle compared to a male with a huge rack that lowered his head to challenge me on a trail below Katahdin on one of my visits there during fall rut season. Placid animals in placid water, they watched us as carefully as we looked at them.

What is our fascination with wildlife? What is the mixture of joy and awe we derive from the presence of other creatures? A few months after returning from Maine, I read the great conservation biologist Edward O. Wilson's book, *Biophillia*, and began gaining some insight. "Humanity," he wrote, "is exalted not because we are so far above other living creatures, but because knowing them well elevates the very concept of life." He saw enchantment with other animals as invigorating poetry and myth because "to the extent that each person can feel like a naturalist, the old excitement of the un-trammeled world will be regained." Thoreau had ignited just such feelings in me with the poetry and myth of his words. I had no doubt that were he alive today, the nineteenth century transcen-dentalist would share a deep and abiding friendship with this soft spoken, bespectacled scientist from his alma mater, Harvard.

Like many primal and organic feelings, delight in wildlife seems only fully expressed in the presence of another person. Alone, it appears, we have no need to communicate the sensation, and as such are less likely to perceive the feelings within us. Looking into Alice's open-hearted smile, her barely containable excitement at the moose, I peered into a mirror of my own emotions. A warm flush of tenderness suddenly coursed through me. The shared moment of wonder urged me to express something deeply endearing for my partner. I longed to gently reach out and stroke her cheek or give her a long, wet kiss. I started to get up, causing the boat to slightly rock. She gave a shout of alarm. Quickly I was back in my seat. With the gesture lost in the awkward scramble over the pile of gear separating us, I kept the thought to myself.

About five miles below Lobster Stream, Moosehorn Stream

enters from the right in a swampy area. Although travelers have stopped and rested at Moosehorn, Ragmuff Stream, just a few miles down river, eclipses it in the minds of Thoreauvian canoeists. For one, it has a commodious campsite on a spit formed by the West Branch and its tributary. But beyond its accommodations, Ragmuff has become a kind of pilgrimage site because Thoreau stopped here three times. He had dinner on this spot twice, coming and going in 1853, and took time to do a little fishing, though he remained mum about his catch. He also bathed in the stream, both in 1853 and 1857. While so doing the second time, he spied a bald eagle overhead.

With all this bathing, Ragmuff has become a kind of Ganges for many paddlers on the West Branch. It's a necessary stop, just as it is to take a drink from Thoreau Spring on Mount Katahdin, though there is no evidence that the great man ever took refreshment there. In light of his current celebrity, it seems odd that Thoreau remained obscure to most Allagash adventurers until the middle of the twentieth century. Today his journeys to the Maine woods are benchmarks for all travelers, and the man's memory is revered.

Thoreau's trips are also now looked upon as a baseline for Maine woods conditions, and often the comparison is deemed unfavorable. We forget that he saw cabins and farms, witnessed fresh stumps and *dri-ki* ("dry killed" dead standing trees drowned by dams), and heard the thud of axes. He noted a squatter's clearing just past Ragmuff. Fortunately, today's woods lack many such intrusions, though there is now some even more pernicious evidence of encroachment by civilization, like roads.

McPhee's canoe-making companion Henri Vaillancourt was so obsessed with Thoreau and finding what the Concord naturalist saw, that in his rabid dash to the next spot he neglected to stop at Ragmuff despite the sad-eyed, bearded image that haunted him. Few know or care that Winthrop also stopped here, caught trout and chub and unsuccessfully sought moose.

Unfortunately, with the Ragmuff site occupied by another party, Alice and I camped our first night among the dense conifers of
Big Island not far downstream. In several places, the ground had
been trampled to a threadbare welcome mat allowing easy erec-
tion of a tent. Blackened fire ring rocks, a few crushed beer cans,
and pieces of burnt aluminum foil were unwanted testimony to
previous nights spent here. Clouds of black flies kept us slapping
ourselves, and until dusk we sought relief under head nets.

Such was the place where I first set up vacation housekeeping
with Alice in a borrowed and battered A-frame nylon tent. It was
not the finest of edifices, but the getaway cottages of new couples
are rarely substantial. Still, the neighborhood was good—quiet,
fragrant with spruce, and redolent with birdsong.

Despite Thoreau's appealing precedent, we found the water
too cold and the bugs too fierce for bathing. Instead, we watched
the evening grow slowly around us. The river glowed silver, then
blushed, tarnished, and finally blackened. The woods became a
tangle of shadows.

Worked beyond exhaustion, we fell asleep without the least desire for amour, setting a pattern for the entire trip regardless of any
intimations of intimacy. I had imagined some kind of unfettered,
primordial romance in the woods, but the lush vegetation proved
no seductive bower. After the muscle wracking labor of each day's
travel we might have missed lovemaking in our hearts, but not in
our loins.

In cloying humidity and with the tent's mosquito netting prov-
ing not fine enough for the no-see-ums, we had a restless night.
Alice had bad dreams that several times startled both of us from
sleep. But for the lullaby gurgle of water running on either side of
the island, we might not have slept at all.

Awakening to a warm morning, we treated ourselves to bacon and
eggs, a luxury that would keep fresh only a few days. Soon enough

we'd find ourselves subject to the dull regimen of oatmeal and granola. Taking our time cooking and eating, the bacon enabled our
meal to assume significance beyond mere tasty nourishment. Bacon has been a staple for almost all Allagash adventurers, and in
light of such a precedent our consumption of the striped ribbons
of meat and fat seemed a species of sacrament. The irresistible in-
cense of the sizzling strips mixed with and seemed as natural here
as the omnipresent odor of spruce.

Soon after breakfast, we were back on the water. The island
faded from view and the river became broad and slow, framed by
margins of lowland. Deliciously fecund scents of mud and decaying vegetation hung in thick humidity. Oppressive heat made us as
languid and lazy as the river.

We spied two moose, including a large bull with a mammoth,
well-palmed rack. Several great blue herons stood elegantly on the
marshy shore, and a bittern stared sphinx-like from one of two
square rock and timber platforms situated midstream. Relics of a
bygone logging era, they now provide a very adequate perch for
birds. Back in the day, the structures were used to help retain the
boom confining the spring drive of newly cut logs.

Black ducks created a commotion on the water, repeatedly taxi-
ing at our advance. Loons dove and hooted to each other as the
river finally widened with almost imperceptible current at its junction with Chesuncook Lake.

Our leisurely paddle along the mud flats dotted with freshwater clams was far from the turbulent excitement that greeted
nineteenth century voyagers. Until 1904, this same stretch of river boiled with whitewater at Rocky Rips and Pine Stream Falls.
"Gnashing rocks with cruel foam . . ." and "great jaws of ugly blackness snapped around us, as if we were introduced to a coterie of
crocodiles," Winthrop wrote of the Rips. Even Eckstorm's experienced guide Reed McPheeters' canoe "broached to, caught and
cracked heavily, coming near swamping." Thoreau walked while his
guide took their boat through.

Our relaxing paddle through the sluggish junction filled with wildlife was very satisfying. Still, something in me longed for those "jaws of ugly blackness" drowned by a dam enlarging Chesuncook.

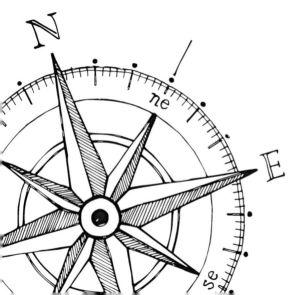

CHESUNCOOK

L ike a curtain rising, the close confines of the river's high banked channel were suddenly gone. Released onto the broad expanse of Chesuncook Lake, Alice and I reflexively drew deep breaths. Impressed by the burst of space, Thoreau found the great stretch of water and sky "liberating and civilizing even."

Surprisingly, I found such dramatic change at the canoe's slow pace more exciting than the rapid cinematic movement of scenery from a speeding car. And it wasn't only alternative surroundings that were stimulating, but our new way of seeing from the boat. While we were truly and literally broadening our horizons on the lake, our unhurried, deliberate progress revealed a whole new world of subtle details we otherwise rarely noticed—tree leaf shapes, cloud movements and sun-sparkle on the water. Our minds had begun adapting to this new tempo, it seemed, in the way eyes adjust to evening's fading light. I turned from my perch in the bow and saw Alice's broad grin. Her eyes twinkled with sun. We were infused with renewed energy.

Chesuncook is an Indian word meaning "a place where many streams empty in." Successive floodings, beginning with dams in the 1840s, have substantially changed its character. Our nineteenth

century compatriots did not see the original Chesuncook, nor do
we see the one that they did. The name probably derives from the
way in which the West Branch, Umbazooksus and Caucomogo-
moc Streams all empty in close proximity at the lake's northern
end. The confluences are much less pronounced today because the
dams enlarging the lake also flooded the river mouths.

In 1764, Joseph Chadwick, a surveyor for the royal governor
of Massachusetts, first described Chesuncook as shallow and mud
bottomed with wide grassy margins. Today trees stand fence-like
along the shore, and in every direction dense forest rolls toward the
horizon. As we entered, a light breeze blew across the water causing it to shimmer and flash.

Most of our predecessors considered the scenic attractions
of Chesuncook "not of a high order," as one put it, except for the
southerly view of mile-high Mount Katahdin and surrounding
summits clustered on the horizon. Thoreau thought the mountains looked like "a cluster of blue fungi of rank growth." We noticed the saw-toothed skyline instantly on paddling onto the lake.
The waterbody seemed enlarged, increased in power by what we
knew to be great mountains appearing so tiny.

"In wilderness," wrote Winthrop, "man makes for man by necessity of human instinct." Indeed, like virtually all travelers to this
part of the world we made directly for Chesuncook Village, a short
paddle south of where the West Branch enters the lake. After traveling between close river banks that passed with every stroke, it
felt as if we were hardly moving forward on the broad water. Still,
it wasn't long before we rounded a nipple of land called Graveyard
Point and moved quickly through the calm behind it to a battered
dock. On shore, a few small boats were turned over. None seemed
to have been recently used.

Chesuncook Village is a small cluster of weatherworn frame
buildings from which no other signs of development can be seen.
First cleared in 1838, it had a population of sixty-five in 1900, blos-

somed to 247 by 1920, and had now dipped to two, according to Dorothy Boone Kidney, a writer who lived summers with her husband at Lock Dam on Chamberlain Lake in the Allagash headwaters. Accessible only by boat or float plane, it is isolated in rolling hills and dense forest on the ragged edge of civilization. It's one of those peaceable places that, in idle hours, you think you might want to live, but realize you never could. Although tiny, it seemed large in its loneliness.

We wandered among the small cottages, kicking up stones along the crooked, narrow ways that passed for streets. We kept an eye out for inhabitants, but all was quiet. Inasmuch as a village is defined not just by buildings, but by people, Chesuncook on this day could hardly be said to have been a village at all. It was a shadow merely, a movie projection.

The center of town featured a tiny church sheathed in white clapboards, but there was no congregation present. The nearby Chesuncook Lake House, still an active hostelry, was a plain frame 1864 farmstead that seemed relatively elegant here in the middle of the woods. Unfortunately, we saw no guests, and innkeepers Bert and Maggie McBurnie were nowhere to be found.

Born in 1931, a trapper's son from Presque Isle, Maine, Bert met Maggie on a trip to her hometown of Paris, France. He's "quite the character" we were told by the guy behind the counter at Sanders Store in Greenville. J. Parker Huber, the Thoreau aficionado and college professor who guides students over the Concord naturalist's travel routes, described running into him in August 1978. The backwoodsman was digging in his yard to unclog the leach field of his dry well. Bert was holding forth on his travels in Europe and Alaska, when Huber "asked him if he ever desired to live anywhere else but Chesuncook. His pipe slipped from one side of his mouth to the other. 'No, never seen anybody I envy,' he replied."

The vegetable and flower gardens were lush and recently cultivated. We spent a few moments sampling the chocolaty perfume of tall, sunflower-like Jerusalem artichokes. The corn appeared small for September. Given the early winters of the region, we wondered whether the stalks would yield much.

It seemed increasingly odd seeing neither visitors nor innkeepers on the neatly groomed grounds, and we began feeling creeped-out, as if we were being watched. I started glancing over my shoulder as if by chance I might see someone looking out a window or from behind a tree. More unusual than finding a village in the woods was discovering a community lacking people. The forest might be devoid of humanity for miles around, but only the vacant village disturbed us, only the village could be said to be empty. After all, in a ghost town you watch for ghosts.

In the unnatural void of Chesuncook Village I first felt how profoundly dependent Alice and I were on each other—for companionship, safety, and the chores of day-to-day living. With a fully loaded boat miles from other people, neither of us could go very far without the other. Canoeing literature is rife with stories of an almost mystical oneness travelers experience with nature. Paddlers often romantically marvel at their unity with the outdoors. Rarely discussed is the union of common effort forced on two people by such a trip. Now we shared strengths and weaknesses, were constrained by necessity to coordinate our wants, our pleasures, and our dislikes just as we must complement each paddle stroke. Turning back, going forward or staying still—it had to be done together.

The day again was hot and humid, but our walk to the small cemetery on Graveyard Point was along a cool, tree shaded path where the ground was moist with condensation. With the village so queerly quiet, a chill overcame me as the headstones came into view. I felt as if we were stepping into a second rate horror film. Suppose we found something really strange, like a graveyard without writing on the stones, or heard the sound of villagers speaking from out of the ground as if in some ersatz Spoon River. I worried that Alice, a newcomer to the deep woods, might become spooked about being isolated in the backcountry. I kept the ghoul-ish thoughts to myself. Fortunately, all we found in the middle of the damp, still forest was a small garden of graves. After hours in bright sun, the diffuse green light was soothing.

Surrounded by the burials of rivermen and babies was Ansel Smith, Chesuncook's most famous citizen. The simple tablet with a curved top was engraved with the compass and square of Free-masonry. He had died on December 30, 1879 at the age of sixty-four years and nine months.

Smith was well known for his hospitality and portage service by lumbermen, explorers and sportsmen when Thoreau arrived in 1853 and spotted "quite a harbor for bateaux and canoes." At the time there were five huts with small clearings on the opposite side of the lake while Smith's was a log house chinked with clay, lichen and moss. Roofed with spruce bark, it had large stone chimneys.

Thoreau described the place as low, about eighty feet long with many spacious apartments. He found it but a slight departure from a hollow tree. About 100 acres were cleared and there was a large garden of root crops. A barn held tons of hay cut in nearby fields for horses and oxen assisting in lumbering. In a blacksmith's shop, animals were shoed and sleds and other equipment fixed.

Winthrop arrived in 1856 to find a former New York bartend-er boiling doughnuts, "of which they had many." Though it might have seemed a strange sight to some, the patrician Winthrop prob-ably felt right at home. Although New Haven born, he had lived in New York City for some time, carefully observing the diverse caval-cade of characters. His tolerance of unusual personalities is evident in *Cecil Dreeme*, one of his three posthumously published novels. It's the story of a girl masquerading as a man among Washington Square artists in order to escape a bad marriage.

About twenty years later, Thomas Sedgwick Steele felt that the building's designer must have had "a mind disordered through indigestion." Perhaps the Hartford jeweler, artist, and writer had too refined an aesthetic sense for such backwoods accommodations. His books are richly illustrated with beautifully detailed, but idealized engravings and wood cuts from his paintings and photographs of landscapes, woodland camps, wildlife, and fishing. Perhaps he was at a loss at having to illustrate such an ungainly structure. Regardless, his time on the Allagash seems to have honed and stimulated his muse, for he would later join the Boston Art Club, study in Paris and travel throughout Europe and North Africa in search of adventure and subjects to depict. Though he gave impressionism a try, much of his later works are still lifes of freshly caught fish and fruit. Given his meticulous artistry, I wasn't surprised that he looked askance at Chesuncook's crude lodgings.

Just after the turn of the century, another traveler was more sanguine about the rough hewn hostelry. He described the place as having typical backwoods accommodations, filled with sportsmen and guides, whose wooden floors had seen the use of caulk boots by lumbermen. Though its appearance, he noted agreeably with others, was anything but inviting, inside he found everything satisfactory.

After traveling to Chesuncook so many times in the pages of books, being here was a species of déjà vu. It was not so much that I could enter the past as it seemed I could see through time. Taking me even deeper was the way in which my fellow travelers' descriptions revealed as much about themselves and their expectations as it did about the places they visited.

None of the buildings Thoreau encountered remain, yet there is still a primitive, unfinished quality to the community. Though the current structures are constructed of more conventional materials, they still have an old timey appearance. Like any pioneer outpost, Chesuncook is ensconced in forest and has no road leading away. "For years," wrote Kidney in 1976, Chesuncook "was a riotous logging town, later a settlement for trappers of mink, beaver, bobcat, and fisher." Afterward, it became a base of operations for hunters and fishermen.

While lunching at Graveyard Point, the wind gradually kicked up. By the time we finished, it was blowing strongly. After being sun-cooked in the hot, bright day, it suddenly became deliciously cool, and goose bumps began multiplying where sweat had recently glistened. When finally we returned to the water, there was no need for paddles. With the wind mercifully behind us, and the water blown to whitecaps, our backs acted like sails and drove us quickly to Umbazooksus Stream. Innovative sails are not unusual on Chesuncook. Winthrop reported using a blanket and McPhee was successful with a large plastic bag.

Pushed by the wind, we quickly crossed the lake's main channel and rounded gigantic Gero Island. Here McPhee's loquacious but shy-eyed Henri Vaillancourt found all he needed for making birch-bark canoes. Seeing four tall paper birches, Vaillancourt instantly headed for shore and decided to camp below them. He also found maple for thwarts and cedar for ribs and gunwales. There were spruce whose roots are for lashing and sewing and pitch for sealing. As we floated past, I imagined Vaillancourt's ecstasy at finding what his Indian predecessors would have considered a perfect spot for canoe making, an outdoor factory site with abundant material and sufficient shade and flat ground. I could almost see him working among the trees.

McPhee's story enabled me to see not merely a forested shore, but a larder of manufacturing materials for a once essential and now almost forgotten craft. The woods became enlarged with meaning. After passing Gero Island, I couldn't help but inventory other places along the Allagash for the possibility of canoe making. The fusion of reading and experience heightened the world around me. Though she understood the trees' usefulness, I seemed unable to convey my sense of deepened awareness to Alice to our mutual frustration. I wish I had brought the slender book with me for her to read.

Of course, Gero wasn't an island when Indians ruled these precincts or even in Thoreau's time. Much of the Umbazooksus they paddled has also disappeared as Chesuncook was enlarged. Dams both created the island and left much of the stream merely an arm of the lake.

We sped across the whitecapped water while loons bobbed in the distance. Trolling a fishing line, we caught a ten-inch trout with lucent orange and yellow stipples. Through the mesh of the net, we watched the glossy creature's labored breathing. Mutual grins grew on our faces, and momentarily I forgot my chapped lips and sunbaked headache. "Trout for dinner?" Alice asked. I smiled and gave a negative shake of my head. We wouldn't have time, I reasoned. Carefully, I removed the hook and tossed the fish back, glad to have briefly encountered something so beautifully wild, yet grateful at not asserting ultimate possession.

Once past the main portion of the lake, we paddled along a stumpy appendage that had once been an entire stream valley with grasses, blue flag iris, willows, and mudflats. It was a world obliterated by flood no less than the one Noah knew, albeit more permanently. Soon we came to a low bridge. By lying flat in the canoe we were able to pass under. Like entering a door into a room, we suddenly found ourselves in the narrow, meadow-edged river of times past. It was "a quiet, somewhat eerie chamber in the woods" that "puts forth a sense of lurking harm," the thoughtful McPhee mused.

UMBAZOOKSUS

We were already growing nervous. We'd talked about it for days, discussed and rehashed our capabilities and weighed them against the difficulties. Tonight we would camp on the friendly shore of Umbazooksus Lake. Tomorrow we'd cross what Steele called "the long dreaded Mud Pond Carry . . . detested by tourists and execrated by guides." Kidney called it "a real man-killer . . . a thick, mucky area that discourages and fatigues canoeists."

On Chesuncook we had felt much as McPhee's party did—tension and verbal tremors at the mention of the infamous portage. I wondered if Alice had the mental stamina and physical strength to make the slog. I'm sure she wondered about me.

We paddled up Umbazooksus Stream toward the isolated, club-shaped lake of the same name where we would find the trailhead on the eastern shore. Greenleaf's 1829 survey describes the Umbazooksus as a "small sluggish stream . . . distinguished only as it rises near the source of the Allagash, and forms the channel of communication between that river and the Penobscot." Such a description makes me wonder if he ever really traveled here. It proved one of the most interesting and beautiful stretches of river Alice and I encountered.

Polis, Thoreau's 1857 guide, said Umbazooksus meant "much meadow river." Between the river's edge and the woods, Thoreau described a margin of meadow between fifty and 200 rods wide where sedges, wool grass, and blue flag grew abundantly. Narrow-leaved willow thrived on higher ground. Dead larches and dri-ki stood along the distant edge of the meadow.

Late in the afternoon, the sun was quickly sinking. We were tired and felt uneasy about the carry we'd face the next day. The weight of isolation hung over this wild, primeval-seeming place. The quiet, meandering stream fringed in bright green vegetation and hemmed in by dense, solemn woods evoked all the foreboding of a dark, fairytale forest. Standing deadwood at the water's edge cast long, twisted shadows across our path. Alice and I hardly spoke, and when we did it was only in broken whispers. We weren't concerned about frightening wildlife or being overheard, for there was no one to hear us. But something in this place enforced quiet, just as even non-believers will speak softly in church.

Wide meadows seemed ideal for moose, but like many others we waited in vain. Though mergansers were afloat ahead of us and a couple herring gulls passed overhead, the birds were queerly silent. A bittern gazed at us from a stump while a Cooper's hawk glided past. We spied a great blue heron stalking fish in the weeds, body taut with intense concentration. Its deliberate, stealthy movements and unblinking observation created a riveting tension that held our attention a full five minutes. It was like watching a movie detective carefully evaluating a clue.

Thoreau saw a nighthawk and a robin here, and another traveler described a flock of red-winged blackbirds hassling a harrier that had ventured close to a nest. Not content to be quiet, Thoreau tested the echo in the meadow, finding it satisfactory. We were in good company.

After all the logging, dams, machinery, and people this fragile, winding stream meadow had endured, it was also eerie, somewhat of a distant echo how much of this place continued as it had always been. Even before Thoreau, Charles T. Jackson's 1830s geological survey had found the stream "sluggish . . . shallow . . . exceedingly crooked," and "almost overgrown," words that still described it well. This unflooded portion seemed to lose itself in vegetation.

I now keenly felt one of the odd contradictions of an Allagash wilderness trip. Despite our being alone at this moment, I was joined by others in an experience transcending space. Bonded with fellow travelers by the continuum of time, I shared their discoveries. Though I mentioned our predecessors to Alice, my excitement, unfortunately, proved not contagious. Nevertheless, we uttered some loud hoots and smiled to each other at the soft boomerang of sound. I was certain I'd heard the slightest hint of Thoreau's voice in the air.

Before long, the wide margin of meadow disappeared, the mucky stream bottom became sandy and stony, and the water grew shallow and fast. Like others, we had to get out and drag the canoe the last bit to Umbazooksus Lake. We passed dead, bleached trees and watched nervously for leeches. On reaching the low dam, we found the sluice gate open. Avoiding the portage, we got out and pushed the canoe up the steel, concrete and earthen structure, quickly under the guillotine-like gate, and into the lake's quiet water.

Umbazooksus Lake is a narrow few miles long, and didn't make much of an impression on our predecessors. Thoreau noted its shallowness and admired the view of Caucomgomoc Mountain. On the southeast shore is a beach of pure bark, a reminder that this was once a major terminal for movement of logs.

Alice and I found the water dark, turbid, and surrounded by an unbroken collar of tightly spaced, gloomy evergreens. Under a sky grown overcast with increasingly large, threatening clouds, the lake seemed oppressive and forbidding. It was an uncomfortably quiet opening in the woods giving off haunted-house premonitions. Though it was something we had avidly sought, solitude weighed heavily. I felt a chilling aloneness, though it was nevertheless intriguing to think there was not another soul for miles.

Exhausted and sticky from a long, muggy day, Alice and I moved slowly, pitching our tent under tall pines a short walk up the carry trail. In 1857, Thoreau found a clearing here with a log cabin at the edge of the trail. Polis went inside and met a Canadian family. The unfortunate man had been blind for a year.

We threw together a hasty dinner of noodles topped with canned cream of asparagus soup and tuna. It was obvious from the compacted and spottily fire-blackened ground that many similar evenings had been spent here for years. The shade was dense, and in the late afternoon overcast the gloom deepened quickly. We were drawn together, perhaps by common childhood fears of dreary remote places that we both felt, but left unexpressed. Sitting in the tent and wrapped in each other's arms, the sound of insects closed around us as night fell.

Long after dark, we were awakened from our sleeping bags by a soft thumping and scratching. A chill shook my body. Instinctively, we sought each other, outlines of shadow in the darkness. Slowly unzipping the tent, I peered uneasily outside. An animal rushed past and startled me. I drew back reflexively and abruptly into the fragile nylon shelter, frightening Alice who let out a suppressed scream. Still shaking, she handed me a flashlight. Much to my delight, the beam lit snowshoe hares hopping through our camp. They nibbled at the ground, wiggled their noses, and leapt to another spot to do the same. I fell backward into the tent hysterical with laughter. Alice began to laugh too, equally uncontrolled. As soon as we grew calm, an exchanged look would send us back into convulsive fits. Only upon clicking off the flashlight after about five minutes did we finally simmer down and fall asleep.

We had found a nicer reality than our imaginations had conjured. "A howling wilderness does not howl," Thoreau noted. "It is the imagination of the traveler that does the howling."

MUD POND CARRY

ud Pond Carry involves no false advertising. It's everything anyone has ever said—none of it good. Perhaps the arduous drudgery of the portage is one of the few things in this world about which there has been little disagreement over generations.

The carry crosses what one traveler called the vertebrae of Maine. You begin in the Penobscot watershed and end in the Allagash. About halfway across this low divide, imperceptible to the naked eye, the waters diverge.

The remoteness and subtlety of the divide, however, did not prevent it from becoming an international flashpoint in the early 1800s. The trouble began with overlapping and ill-defined competing royal grants of land early in the seventeenth century that confused the boundary between Maine and Canada. The Treaty of Ghent, which concluded the War of 1812, set up a commission to resolve the dispute. After several years, the commissioners failed and later arbitration by the King of the Netherlands was also unsuccessful. With increasing settlement and hunger for timber on both sides of the border (wherever it was) tensions mounted leading to what has been dubbed the bloodless Aroostook War. Maine dispatched troops and quickly constructed Forts Kent and Fairfield, and New Brunswick marshaled soldiers along the St. John. Diplomacy eventually prevailed, and in 1842 negotiations between Daniel Webster and Lord Ashburton resulted in a treaty that put the long simmering dispute to rest.

Gazing around me at the dark, foreboding woods, it was hard to believe that I was about to cross an unmarked line that once concerned great historical figures and played on the world stage. My sights were considerably lower. I just wanted to make it over the carry with as little gut-wrenching difficulty as possible.

The mile and three-quarter carry has been an artery of travel for Native Americans, explorers, lumbermen, and sportsmen since time immemorial. Feet from all those centuries have worn a path well over a foot into the forest floor. Lucius Hubbard, the Boston lawyer turned Michigan geologist, observed that the carry "in many places has the appearance of the bed of a brook, with water and mud enough to float a canoe." Steele wrote that his party sank to their knees in mud, and his guides claimed that there was water enough to drag their boats in some seasons. He also claimed to have found a twelve-inch square pool of water along the trail which held a foot-long trout. At the turn of the century, G. Smith Stanton, whose other books ranged from describing New York city apartment living to fifteen years as a stockman and livestock shipper on the great plains, not only saw nine moose at the carry, but the odd sight of "a party of New Yorkers among which were several ladies."

Perhaps the most curious experience on the Mud Pond Carry was had by Thoreau who called it a "loosely paved gutter." He and his friend Ed Hoar were clearly not enjoying the passage, so Polis (who "said that this was the wettest carry in the State") suggested they take a parallel route that was drier, but eventually reconnected with the main trail. Confused by numerous logging and animal paths, the two were quickly lost. Attacked by voracious black flies, bushwhacking through thickets, and wading knee deep in mud they finally reached the shore of Chamberlain Lake without ever seeing Mud Pond. When eventually they caught up with Polis, he was surprised, saying only that their losing their way was "strange." "I would not have missed that walk for a good deal," Thoreau wrote, typically enjoying being at variance with common perceptions.

Without gear to haul, Mud Pond Carry might almost be a pleasant walk. The spruce forest emanates a soothing green light and the surrounding ground is carpeted with thick, spongy moss. The greenery is iridescent, the damp odors rich and cooling. There were many large moose prints in the mud, and two antic spruce grouse, the brown-mottled chicken of the north woods, ran comically ahead of us for some distance as we progressed up the path.

Between the two of us, we made five trips over the trail. It was wet and slick, and even in this dry season there were boggy places where you could sink to the ankles, hear a sucking sound as you lifted your foot and come up without a sneaker. Hauling the boat was the final and worst crossing. With arms over my head to stabilize the canoe on my shoulders, lines of sweat ran in ticklish trickles down my neck, chest, and back while the rest of me ached from the awkward seventy-eight pound weight. I was helpless against insects buzzing around my head, and my heart beat hard and echoed in my ears.

In desperation lest both body and mind give out, I broke into song at the top of my lungs. These were no French work tunes once uttered by the fur-trapping Canadian voyageurs, but a medley of numbers by Al Jolson, Cole Porter, Woody Guthrie, Bob Dylan, and the Beatles. Imagine being miles from civilization and hearing a booming voice singing "Toot, Toot, Tootsie" and "Pretty Boy Floyd" and "Mr. Tambourine Man." I couldn't carry a tune in a bucket, but the boat over my head resonated like a shower stall and my voice seemed almost pleasing to me. Alice was very brave, but it was either withstand my croaky off-key voice or carry the canoe.

The real trick was balancing the sixteen-foot boat rubbing hard on my shoulders while dancing around the rocks and muddy spots and simultaneously keeping down enough to avoid low hanging branches. It was not easy with my vision obscured by the canoe over my head. Alice called the dance steps while I moved in fits and starts under the boat.

There was a time when the Mud Pond Carry was not so arduous. In the early twentieth century, there was a team and wagon available at Umbazooksus Lake to get visitors and their gear across. In the late nineteenth century, travelers could avoid Umazooksus Lake altogether by taking Ansel Smith's portage service from a point on Umbazooksus Stream. It was six miles long and accomplished by use of two horses attached to a sled-like vehicle on which the gear was carried. Hubbard wrote that Smith charged $6 and had made $120 in two months. Some who made the three hour trip complained bitterly about the price. Had they tried the Mud Pond Carry, they gladly would have paid twice as much.

The wind picked up in fickle, shifting gusts as we neared the end of the trail, several times almost ripping the boat from my hands. Lumpy, charcoal-colored clouds dampened the day to almost twilight. Suddenly a thunder boom resounded in the woods and a bolt of electricity shattered the darkness. Fighting gusty wind and pelted with quarter-sized drops of rain as thick as a waterfall, I couldn't see and threw off the boat. With the trees around us shaking wildly, we huddled beneath a tarp, blue-lipped, shivering, and wet until the storm passed.

Rain hit the thin sheet of plastic with loud, percussive drops and the violent wind tried ripping it from our hands. But despite discomfort and inconvenience, the storm enforced a beneficial rest. Though she didn't have to carry the canoe, I could see my own exhaustion echoed in Alice's face where bug bites and a few scratches marred the smile she briefly flashed as she caught me looking at her.

Arrival at Mud Pond gave no relief from the overwhelming sense of gloomy solitude that followed us, or from our struggle to make progress. From the shore we saw no sign of man save the carry trail on which we had just traveled. The water was low, and a wide belt of muck surrounded the pond like a moat. Sinking to our knees in the oozing gumbo as we dragged the canoe to the water's edge, we built a puncheon of sticks and stones so we could load the gear. By the time everything was aboard, the makeshift pier had sunk and was no longer visible. Again, we were up to our knees in mud. Using our paddles, it took some vigorous polling to get afloat.

No one has ever recorded enjoying Mud Pond. I suppose it's not easy to fall in love with a slowly dying lake already halfway to becoming a swamp. It's been called "dismal," two miles of uninteresting scenery, and an understated "uninviting."

The mocha water of Mud Pond was no more than a few feet deep and weeds grew even in the middle. It was surrounded by tall evergreens and low, light-green wetlands. Perhaps it's good Mud Pond has always been just a place to pass through, for its beauty lies in its insularity. I was exhilarated at being at the center of a place unglamorous and inhospitable. Here was a corner of the world where you could never live, where people would always be strangers, a place no one would ever seek out.

Having finished the strenuous carry, we reveled in being afloat again. In a slight breeze, sweat and rain evaporated from my clothing and offered cool refreshment. Alice's ginger curls and freckles sparkled in the sunshine. We were all smiles. Real progress at last.

Our rapture was cut short when we unexpectedly found ourselves stuck on the bottom about 125 feet from our destined shore. Again using our paddles as poles, with strenuous effort we made another thirty-five feet or so in just a few inches of water. I thought to get out and pull the canoe, but when I sank my sixty-inch paddle to the hilt in the bottom ooze without touching hard ground, I knew an alternative was needed. Sinuous leeches swarmed toward the planted shaft. The moist, dank odor of muck wafted on the breeze.

There we sat in the baking sun almost within spitting distance of shore, but unable to budge. Trapped in our boat, the lake seemed to contract around us, the forest appeared darker, menacing.

For about fifteen minutes, we haggled over a way out. In the deep mud there was no way to lighten the boat by wading gear to shore. We thought about redistributing the weight, but that seemed pointless. With grunting effort we tried poling in concert from opposite sides and from the same side to no avail. Hot and tired, spattered with mud, we began snapping at each other, questioning the whole trip in begrudging tones.

My back ached from carrying the canoe and straining to push the boat with my paddle. Alice's ideas were starting to get on my nerves. In jest, I suggested that a canal ought to be dug from Umbazooksus to Chamberlain Lake. Instantly we recognized a solution.

Using my paddle, I dug a small channel in front of the boat and let it fill with a couple inches of coffee-colored water. With vigorous poling, the additional liquid provided just enough lubrication to allow tediously slow progress, foot by foot. For the first time I was glad to have an oversized plastic paddle, rather that the elegant, handcrafted sugar maple one Thoreau used.

After some time, and with sore arms, we at last reached the pond outflow which was dammed with battered old logs. We thought ourselves uniquely clever until I later reread Steele's account of his second journey. He had done the same thing.

Mud Brook, the pond's outlet, is a twisting, rocky little stream curling through unkempt woods. It's been called somewhat of a canal from centuries of boaters removing rocks and throwing them on shore. If so, it's a shallow and contorted canal. As far as I could tell, it never has enough water to float a fully loaded canoe. We paddled just a minute and dragged the boat the rest of the way.

My body felt as heavy as the canoe. In my exhaustion, I hardly distinguished between them. Shoving the boat became automatic, a reflex. I no longer thought about what I was doing. Together, Alice and I pushed and pulled around rocks and over half submerged logs as we stumbled over slippery stones and sharp sticks. After the carry and struggling through Mud Pond, we were physically and mentally spent. Splashing drunkenly through the water, we forced the loaded boat through a pinball course of obstacles like a single frenzied animal. I was amazed at Alice's stamina. But exhaustion and a focused purpose created an unfaltering will. When finally we exited Mud Brook, I could only think how queer it was to see clear water running from Mud Pond.

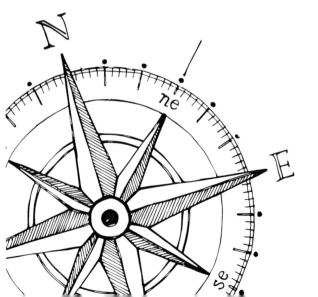

CHAMBERLAIN LAKE

We entered Chamberlain Lake through a marshy cove filled with long dead, ghostly silver trees. The cove is a sort of ante-chamber separating the turbid waters above from the clear depths of Maine's second largest body of freshwater. We spotted a great blue heron and frightened a flock of black ducks. "The old grey stumps scattered about," wrote the artsy Steele as if he were painting in words rather than his usual oils, "seemed like storm-beaten tombstones which marked the resting places of perished souls, and the naked, bleached forms of the trees in a palisade like sentinel skeletons guarding a death ground."

After the miserable struggle across Mud Pond in heat and thick humidity, I, like Thoreau, was relieved at the sight of Chamberlain with its spacious expanse, solid shore and clear water. I delighted in a chilling bath, ridding myself of muddy smears decorating my body like a long-time sailor's tattoos.

We camped on the sandy beach near where we entered the lake. It was probably not far from the spot where Steele in the 1880s saw an "immense" bull caribou dart into the woods, an animal not seen in these parts for nearly a century. Polis thought the dead trees caused by the dams had frightened off the once abundant ungulates. "No likum stump," Thoreau recorded him saying, "— when he sees that he scared."

The broad vistas were as invigorating as the cold water. We could see a far and focused distance up and down the relatively narrow, fourteen-mile-long lake. It was as if we'd suddenly been given sight in yet another dimension. The sky was vast, lit like a great planetarium, its light slowly going from yellow to pink, then to red, and finally purple before darkening with needle points of starlight. We ate but a couple granola bars and fell asleep instantly, our muscles aching with exhaustion.

Loons called across the water throughout the night, interrupting our sleep with their hauntingly weird cries. As we lay awake listening to the birds between bouts of deep snoozing, moose would slosh their way through the shallows in front of the tent. Although moose are the most heralded creature of the Maine woods, no animal—not moose, bear, nor beaver—has caused as much introspection and held the imagination as magnetically as the loon. What is the mystery that evokes such deep feeling? What universal chord is struck? What power does this bird have over us?

Loons are a kind of overweight, maniacal duck. Their bills are dagger-like for snaring fish, they have dark hooded heads, and black backs flecked with white. Typically you see them calmly bobbing on the water and then suddenly darting beneath the surface like a fish-seeking torpedo. When they emerge again, it's usually distant from where they dove. Although expert swimmers, loons walk awkwardly on terra firma and require the longest of watery runways to attain flight. Landing is somewhat of a belly flop. Their most remarkable attribute is an almost insanely human laugh.

Loons are said to make several distinctive sounds—a wail, tremolo, yodel, and hoot. Their vocalizations have been likened to ghosts, demonic laughter, babies crying, and wolves calling. Chipewyans thought the sound was a portent of death, some have said, and Crees heard the cry of a warrior denied entry into heaven.

With an attention to detail that must have served him well in both legal and scientific careers, Hubbard attempted to analyze these calls and place them in musical notation. Still, he was mystified as to why he found the sounds so haunting. He ascribed many human attributes to the bird, finding its notes "more significant than those of many other birds, at times merry, tender, dreary, or full of fear, but almost always musical." Thoreau, too, was at a loss to describe his attraction. "This of the loon," he wrote, "—I do not mean its laugh, but its looning—is a long-drawn call, as it were, sometimes singularly human to my ear,—hoo-hoo-ooo. . . ."

When first awakened to the loon's laughter, I thought I'd been startled by my own dream. Alice was bolt upright in her sleeping bag when I opened my eyes. We looked at each other in the soft, water reflected moonlight and enjoyed a few quiet loon-like laughs between us. It seemed as if the woods themselves were calling. It was a speaking in tongues—simultaneously utterances of pure joy and sorrow.

Among the most primitive of birds, perhaps some primordial aspect to the sound resonates deep in the subconscious of the human psyche finding something not generally accessible. Despite all the sounds of technological wizardry, there is still nothing that affects us like that ancient bird with its iridescent greenish-black head and piercing red eye.

It was 46 degrees when we awoke at 5:30 with a light wind riffling the water. The sky grew slowly pink, highlighting large, puffy clouds. Loons still echoed in the distance. Gazing at the broad expanse of water, I felt a joyous freedom rise in me. I was eager to jump into the day even as I savored the quiet dawn. My imagination soared at the thought that we were now firmly on the headwaters of the Allagash. We shoved off as rosiness faded from the sky.

The lake's English name memorializes a farming family that settled here in the 1840s. *Apmoojenegamook*, meaning "cross lake," is the Indian moniker since traditionally its width was paddled across to reach Eagle Lake rather its fourteen-mile length. The Indian name was descriptive of what Alice and I had to accomplish, since the most direct route to the Allagash River is to paddle up the lake a few miles and then cross over to Lock Dam where a small stream connects with Eagle Lake.

Regardless of the aptness of Indian names, Stanton opined that the native "names of the lakes and streams in Maine can stand cropping off a syllable or two with a certainty that there will be plenty left." It seems a rather odd statement for a man raised in a household where the rights and culture of blacks, women, and downtrodden people were vigorously defended. No doubt the names are long and awkward on an English speaking tongue. But just such attributes provide an inspiriting, wonderful music that takes me even further into this wild country. Such names reminded me of Thoreau's delight in Polis' Indian accent as "wild and refreshing," like "wind among the pines, or the booming surf on the shore."

Polis told Thoreau that loons calling were a sign of wind. Indeed, we began the day with a slight headwind that increased steadily until paddling went from difficult to grueling. Whitecaps were soon on the water and we hugged the shore where small points of land deflected the stiffest gusts. Our arms quickly became sore. Having to grip the paddles tightly, our hands tingled from loss of circulation. Unable to stop while on the water lest the wind push us broadside and we lose what progress we'd made, we landed to rest at Ellis Brook, frightening three deer as we approached. While we sat on shore, the wind only increased in velocity. Though our arms were tired and numb, we didn't rest long.

The narrow, finger-shaped lake was a wind tunnel, becoming threatening with fierce foaming whitecaps and three-foot swells.

Crossing directly to Lock Dam would have been foolhardy. Not only might we be swamped, but the wind would have pushed us far down the lake even as we made progress to the opposite side. After another brief respite on shore, we decided to paddle toward a point above Lock Dam and then head down and across on an angle.

We paddled hard, trying to get some weigh-on before hitting mid lake, which was frothing with heavy whitewater. Wind kept trying to push us broadside, and in the stern I was hard pressed to take compensating strokes for fear we would lose what little forward momentum we'd gained. I swore at the top of my lungs, but the sound quickly dissipated in the wind. In the bow, Alice put all her strength and weight into each stroke. I could see her body shaking with effort as her long hair unraveled from a bandana and blew in her face obscuring her vision. My arms pulsated with pain and stiffness, and it felt as if the lake was sucking the paddle from my hands. Several waves crashed over the bow and onto my legs, leaving a couple inches of cold water sloshing at our feet. Chamberlain became a violent demon. "A wave will gently creep up the side of the canoe," Thoreau observed, "and fill your lap, like a monster deliberately covering you with its slime before it swallows you." I wanted to reach for the bailer, but couldn't sacrifice a single paddle stroke.

We yelled words of encouragement to each other and talked up our progress, but inside I felt helpless, overpowered. It seemed as if we were pushing against a wall. I grunted with effort at each stroke. My hands blistered. The blisters broke and my flesh stung as if I'd rubbed salt into the raw spots. Our chatter became more frequent, devolved into mere sounds signifying mutual effort. Our lives now literally depended on working together, on common strength. The labor somehow resulted in more than the sum of our individual abilities. Water and wind had contrived an entirely new entity. Two people in a canoe were a single organism.

My muscles began cramping and my strength gave way as we reached middle ground where several gusts almost swept me from the canoe. Wind whistling and chattering in my ears seemed like a taunt. With Alice's strength sapped and me unable to hold the course from the stern any longer, we angled further down wind. Choppy water snapped at the boat, and gusts clawed viciously. Every canoe length of progress was hard fought, and our plan to reach the lake's east side felt like a grand military strategy reduced to hand-to-hand combat. Finally, we neared the intended shore, but about a mile below Lock Dam.

Approaching land, we hopped waist high into the frigid lake. Using the last of our strength, we kept the canoe, half filled with water, from being battered on the rocks by onrushing surf. At last rolling with the rhythm of a large breaker like surfers, we shoved the boat onto dry ground, collapsing on sun-warmed slabs of stone and emptying the lake from our shoes. My hands were bleeding, pulsing with pain.

Out in the middle of Chamberlain we spotted a ranger's power boat tossed like a toy though it was titanic compared with our canoe. Even its powerful engine struggled with the wind. Without our notice, we surmised, it had been dispatched for a rescue in case we had swamped or capsized.

The endless sky punctuated with cauliflower clouds floating above the angry, whitecapped lake was breathtaking. I felt not only drained of energy, but tiny. Katahdin and surrounding mountains were blue saw-tooth silhouettes on the southern horizon. I remembered Thoreau's sense of awe when the same view caught his eye. The mountain, Thoreau, and I were somehow connected in a way I couldn't quite fully grasp, though it felt almost palpable. Dodging rocks and driftwood and passing rugged slate ledges pocked with gray, green, and orange lichen, we haltingly walked the canoe up to Lock Dam in the relentless surf.

Vexing wind on Chamberlain never changes. Thoreau had to wait out the chop and swells, and McPhee was moved to write that the human race was linked by its common hatred of wind. He supposed the Indians called the lake Apmoojenegamook knowing no sane person would attempt to paddle the long way on this "whistling groove whose waves stand up like the teeth of a saw."

Although many nineteenth century travelers delighted in the distant view of Katahdin, they often found the lake unsightly because lined with driftwood and dead trees, making the shore virtually inaccessible. Today the water's edge is generally rocky and gravelly with occasional pieces of driftwood.

The drowned trees are largely gone now, but the cause of their demise, Lock Dam, remains. In 1841, the dam was built at Chamberlain's north flowing outlet stream to Eagle Lake. A second dam was built at the south end of Telos Lake (which is connected to Chamberlain on the south). Combined with a 500-foot cut dug from Telos to the East Branch of the Penobscot, the raised water levels enabled logs cut in the headwaters of the Allagash to flow south to Bangor's mills. Another dam, which no longer exists, was built on Chamberlain's outlet stream near where it enters Eagle Lake. It was used in combination with Lock Dam like a transportation canal lock system. Logs on lower Eagle Lake were towed between the dams, the water level raised, and the logs then pulled out onto higher Chamberlain.

Allagash logging has a colorful history. Fortunes were won and lost. A vigilante war was fought over the cost of sending logs through Telos Cut, and Canadian loggers tried to blow up Lock Dam, believing the diversion left the St. John River too dry to float their own logs.

We arrived at Lock Dam wet and exhausted, though it was only noon. We thought of camping on the south side where Thoreau had dinner in July 1857. But a little north of the dam was a small cabin shingled in green asphalt, the summer residence of dam tenders Dorothy and Milford Kidney. Observing our bedraggled appearance, Milford called to us and we gladly accepted an invitation to come inside and warm up by the old cook stove. With its gray-painted floor, rustic table, two beds (over one of which was a 12-gauge shotgun), black iron sink, simple wooden chairs and other plain furniture, entering their cabin was like stepping into a Norman Rockwell painting.

The elderly, white-haired couple had been posted here for twenty-six summers. They were welcoming and sweet with voices soft and reassuring. In true Thoreauvian manner, they "distilled living to a basic simplicity," I later read in a book Dorothy had written. "The living has not only shaped us but has shaped our total outlook on life as well. We have become part of the forest, and the forest . . . has become in a very real sense a part of us," she reasoned. We delighted in their rapid and easy talk while devouring Dorothy's fresh-baked muffins. Milford gave me a couple large bandages for my hands which he affixed with adhesive tape. They were the all-American grandparents.

Milford kept an eye on the waterway for the state and managed the dam for the East Branch Improvement Company. Retired from typewriter and other business machine sales jobs, he effervesced with stories of fishing and camping. He was a dry fly fisherman who had a preference for large grasshoppers, but was not above using worms or slices of chub when the fish weren't rising. She chimed in with anecdotes about bears, moose and foxes, and berry picking expeditions.

Over the years, the couple had played genial host to hundreds of windbound canoeists, given directions, helped lost and capsized paddlers, and dealt with medical emergencies of all sorts. Milford told us you could find dry wood in a wet forest by chopping away at the underside of downed trees. Birch bark would ignite under a match in practically any conditions. Dorothy talked about their private "zoo" of tame deer, squirrels and other animals, and showed us samples from her "driftwood museum."

Dorothy is a writer with several volumes to her credit, including a novel, children's stories, books of religious inspiration and, of course, tales of her life with Milford in the backcountry. Here at the only bookstore on the Allagash, we bought a copy of *A Home in the Wilderness.* Her Allagash books were the most popular, filled with a mixture of homilies, recipes, anecdotes, and parental-like advice along with stories of hapless campers and cute animals. Sometimes, she said, she wrote letters on birch bark, mailing them in envelopes of the same material.

The weather, Dorothy noted, was the most critical element in forming visitors' impressions of the Allagash. "Our lake," I read later that day in the book we purchased, "is never just a lake."

> It is a mirror of moods and can change daily, often hourly, from a placid pond without a ripple to a snarling beast with waves eight feet high. Fog shrouded, it can be an eerie gray specter right out of a Gothic novel. In bright sunlight, its smooth surface sparkles like a dazzling sequined gown. It not only is a reflector of moods but of colors as well. It becomes frighteningly black when a storm is approaching. Other times it is sun-splashed to blinding brilliance on a bright day.

I wanted to see more of this dominant, moody water body and head south along the shore a few miles to visit Chamberlain Farm as Thoreau had done. In his time, the farm provisioned the logging industry, growing oats and hay for workhorses and apples, potatoes, and other vegetables. Cattle and sheep grazed on the slopes above the water. Just as Thoreau was interested in visiting Chesuncook's Ansel Smith "to see how a pioneer lived on this side of the country," so was I eager to explore Chamberlain Farm. Although farming and the spacious fields of Thoreau's day were long gone, just south of it were Nugent's Camps, a cluster of guest cabins and the home of Al "Nuge" and Patty Nugent. They had come as pioneers on a log raft in 1936, escaping the Depression and seeking a simple existence free of utility bills, mortgages, and other entanglements. The first year, they built a hut of driftwood and planted a garden and hunted and fished to feed themselves.

Nugent hospitality was legendary, and everyone who knew anything about Chamberlain Lake advised me to visit, including the Kidney's. Al had passed away in 1978, but seventy-eight year-old Patty was still sprightly, greeting visitors, cooking her famous pies, and telling stories that folks said would have you on the edge of your seat. Dorothy was full of tales about their neighbor, including one about the time Patty shot a bear digging around the dump behind her cabin.

Stanton was first to mention a tender at Lock Dam, the polished New Yorker quipping that like all night watchmen he retired at nightfall. Not long before Alice and I paid them a visit, Thoreauvian tour guide J. Parker Huber found that "together the Kidneys express a deep love for the wilderness, humanity, simplicity, God and each other." Essayist Edward Hoagland, guided in the early 1970s by old-time Allagash hand Fred King, noted with disdain that "the lock tender himself was a summer visitor, a white-haired salesman with an ulcer whose wife wrote children's books." Regardless that they see the same places and people, travelers clearly bring many different things to the Allagash.

When sufficiently warmed, dried and cheered, we bid goodbye to the Kidneys and returned to our canoe and gear to assess our prospects. Maybe it was the last few days of living in close proximity, or the hard-fought effort crossing the lake, but I now felt a rush of emotion drawing me closer to Alice. The canoe pressured us into a unit. The intensity of events seemed to have the effect of time, and our history together suddenly expanded beyond mere count of days. Here we were known only as a couple, and that seemed to tighten our bond. I felt it, saw it in the way Alice walked beside me, the warmth in her smile, and the gentle way she pumped my sore hand as we strolled back to the boat. Looking at a loving elderly couple long grown into each other's ways, I thought I caught a glimpse of Alice and me thirty years hence.

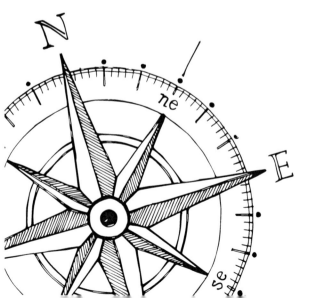

EAGLE AND CHURCHILL

t some length we considered whether to camp at Lock Dam, venture up the lake to Chamberlain Farm, or continue to Eagle Lake. We were not alone. A similar debate raged with all the serious deliberation of a major corporate venture among an unlikely assembly of about a dozen people waiting out the tireless gale just beyond the Kidney's front yard. Braced against the wind while waves crashed rhythmically on shore were a craggy-faced guide and his well-fleshed sport, a gaggle of juvenile delinquents with chaperones, and a family with two young children.

Since it was only just past lunchtime and Milford and the crusty guide in a green and black buffalo plaid shirt assured us that Eagle was never as windy as Chamberlain, Alice wanted to press on. She seemed eager to get as far along toward the confluence with the St. John as possible and I wondered whether she was getting tired of the woods, the strenuous effort, or me. I agreed that there was no way we could continue up Chamberlain in the strong wind and heavy water, but she seemed piqued when I suggested that we wait out the blow and camp at Lock Dam so we could make our way to Nugent's in the morning. Patty Nugent, I explained, was the last link to the pioneering spirit on the Allagash. I pushed her almost to the point of a shouting argument, not hard to achieve given our physical discomfort the past couple days. She wasn't budging and pushed right back.

We were wasting time, Alice said pointedly, and the wind might not let up for days. There was no way she was going to stay trapped at Lock Dam. "This may be your idea of a good time," she told me waving a finger, "but I want to get going. I don't care about meeting some old woman." She sounded downright nasty, condescending. She acted as if I'd proposed visiting an old girlfriend or going to a strip club. It was a personality trait I hadn't before witnessed.

I couldn't predict the wind. She was right about that. In contemplating spending the next week inescapably close to someone hopelessly pissed off at me, I made the only reasonable decision. I gave in. The tenderness I felt holding hands as we left the Kidney's cabin suddenly evaporated. For the first time I felt the need for a shower.

Given her age, I'd probably given up the only chance I'd ever get to meet and share a cup of coffee with the fabled Patty Nugent. I consoled myself by remembering that Thoreau arrived late at Chamberlain Farm and didn't get to see much. The place was "no doubt a cheerful opening in the woods, but such was the lateness of the hour that it left but a dusky impression on my mind," he wrote. Needing additional provisions, he was disappointed that "they were unwilling to spare more than four pounds of brown sugar," though the price of twenty cents a pound was favorable so far from civilization.

Milford opened the dam gates, which he called "the keys to paradise," and we put our canoe into the narrow corridor of Chamberlain's outlet stream. Water gushed from the conduits as if from a fire hydrant. The hurried flow echoed in the stream's tight valley and once again we found ourselves afloat, dropping about fifteen feet in the roughly half mile to Eagle Lake, cruising over metamorphosed sedimentary rocks more than 500 million years old.

Like Thoreau, we found it odd that such a tiny stream should connect two huge water bodies. "It is remarkable," he wrote, "how little these important gates to a lake are blazoned. There is no triumphal arch over the modest inlet or outlet, but at some undistinguished point it trickles in or out through the uninterrupted forest, almost as through a sponge." Thoreau portaged around the second dam where some have reported good fishing. Milford mentioned some timbers still projecting from the long-gone lower structure, but we didn't notice them.

Thoreau found Eagle Lake's shore "ragged and unsightly" owing to flooding caused by Churchill Dam to the north. Although also long and somewhat narrow, Eagle is generally considered more attractive because its irregular shoreline is less rigid than Chamberlain's. Eagle is also broader, has hillier surroundings and boasts several islands. It often delights those seeking isolation as deeper in the woods than probably any point along the Allagash. Large white pines stand out on nearby slopes, and some of them, Milford said, were 120 feet tall. One visitor found the "moosier swards by the water" enchanting.

We entered Eagle Lake at Martin Cove. The wind was moderate, giving us hope the paddle ahead would be less tormenting. We'd been told that the lake was subject to unpredictable fits of calm. Still, we embarked with great trepidation.

Some paddlers have reported scaring as many as forty to fifty mergansers to flight on entering the cove. They've spotted terns, black ducks, loons, and osprey flying overhead. Unfortunately, when we started paddling any waterfowl were probably waiting out the blow in snug harbors.

Moving from the cove's protection, the wind hit us like an eighteen-wheeler passing at highway speed. Soon, conditions were as bad as ever. Rounding a point, we again crashed into whitecaps and were almost pushed broadside and swamped. Cedars, spruce, birch, and firs waved wildly along the shore. Why, I wondered, hadn't I insisted on camping at Lock Dam. I was angry at myself for having given up.

Reaching the next neck of land required crossing a second, larger cove where the wind bore down at us with more force than I've ever experienced in a canoe. Once again we pushed as hard as muscles could endure. I felt a giddy rush of adrenaline even as I felt the ache of exertion and sharp pain in my blistered hands. Paddling was oppressively arduous, and the water again incessantly grasped for the paddle. My heart sank as I watched the shore toward which we headed slowly recede no matter how hard we tried to move ahead. It was anguishing, a numbing agony. I cursed at the top of my lungs in an attempt to concentrate. Alice cursed too. We were a floating engine of blasphemy.

I feared we would capsize. Perhaps such dread put something extra in my stroke. Though the wind continued steadily and I felt my arms weaken, we slowly began making progress. Fifteen minutes later, we lay exhausted on a point of land jutting into the lake just south of Pillsbury Island. We munched on chocolate and tried regaining our strength. After our snack, we lined the boat, floating it on the water in rough surf while we moved along the shore with bow and stern lines held in our hands. At last in the shelter of the island, we got into the canoe and with a short burst of hard paddling, made it to the Thoreau campsite halfway up its western side.

Although Thoreau stopped for dinner on Pillsbury Island, he did so at the southern tip, never setting foot on the area that bears his name. It was the furthest he traveled on Allagash waters. He found the island elevated, densely wooded, and edged in rock. So it remains. Thoreau spent his time botanizing, recording over a dozen wildflower species. Among them were rough cinquefoil, mad-dog skullcap, tradescant's aster, heal-all, and sheep sorrel.

As we set up our tent, the wind caught it like a sail. The gusts grew. A fierce sough rushing through the trees filled the air, while the sound of breakers crashing on the shore reverberated in my chest. Like Thoreau, we discovered that the wind "created such a sea that we found ourselves prisoners on the island." Poor Alice sat in the tent for almost an hour trying to brush the windblown knots out of her hair. A silver moon followed a yellow sunset.

That evening, we spent a couple hours around the flickering light of a campfire chatting with two broad-shouldered and genial Canadians with whom we were inmates. Over a couple Sierra cups of their peaty single-malt Scotch we jawed about the weather, fishing, canoes, food, and an outdoor life's other simple pleasures. With the fire crackling, the wind constantly rushing, and the darkness deep around us I felt thrown back to a more primitive time when we all might have been woodsmen eking out our living from the forest. Their stubble bearded faces, rough wool clothing, and dirt-creased, callused hands made the law practice they spoke of in Halifax seem as improbable as it was distant. I tried not to let their dinner of canned frog's legs and radiation-preserved veal marsala trouble my romantic image.

It all seemed simple enough, the small talk of an evening meal. Yet in this ordinary conversation was the germ of something different. Again, Alice and I were a couple. Our opinions, tastes and feelings vibrated against the background of each other. In the eyes of people who had never met us alone, we were no longer just ourselves. We were a corporate entity. At home, among friends who knew us individually, I hadn't felt this new identity. After our disagreement at Lock Dam, I had mixed feelings. A glance at Alice told me she did as well.

Before turning in for the night, I walked with my flashlight to the freshly limed outhouse. The walls inside held a wealth of graffiti in both prose and verse, and I moved my light around and read as I did my business. Written in bold black letters on my left was the inscription "H.D. Thoreau—1857." I laughed heartily, probably more than merited. Some of the afternoon's tension subsided.

Returning to the tent, I snuggled down into my sleeping bag. With my light properly angled, I got out a small spiral notebook and a pen (sealed tightly in four clear plastic bags) to jot down my thoughts for the day, as had been my habit each evening. They were cryptic notes. On my return home, I'd expand them in the journal I'd kept for several years.

"What are you writing about," Alice asked with a bare hint of interrogator's edge. Having thought her asleep, she surprised me. It was her first inquiry about my note taking, a long-time habit she'd often witnessed.

"Just about what we saw today," I answered neutrally.

"Like what?" Suddenly I felt self-conscious. It was as if she were trying to break into my safe deposit box. I suspected she really wanted to know if I was taking revenge in words over our argument at the dam.

"Stuff like the wind and hard paddling, meeting the Kidneys, the trees we saw, the clouds."

"That's all?"

"Yeah, that's about it," I guess I lied—but just a little. She rolled over with a grunt and went to sleep.

Determined to beat the wind, we awoke at five o'clock the next morning and with a breakfast of only a couple granola bars, were on the water by six. Eagle was as smooth as cellophane wrapped tightly over the mouth of a jar. The water reflected sunrise in yellows and pinks. I could hardly believe this was the same lake where just yesterday roller after whitecapped roller slammed onto the shore. It was as if hilly surroundings had become a plain over night. The entire character of the place had changed.

Ripples around the canoe reflected the day's fresh sunlight, and we felt almost manic high spirits on finding the lake in an early morning calm. It was liberating to realize how irresistibly and profoundly the weather set my moods, just as Dorothy had said. I had broken loose of the regular nine-to-five rhythms of my job and become tied to something more hypnotic and heart-stirring. The canoe glided easily, as if the lake were a buttered glass platter. It felt absurdly easy. We spotted a golden-crowned kinglet and a black-throated green warbler.

A short distance up the western side, we came to the most visited site on the Allagash. Pieces of rusted metal—bolts, screws, wires and gears—were strewn about the shallow water and marshy shore. A tramway starting here was built in 1902 and 1903 and once transported logs over the 3,000-foot-long height of land between Eagle and Chamberlain Lakes. Once the logs made it to Chamberlain on this "moving sidewalk," as Stanton termed it in 1905 when it was fully operating, they were boomed and towed down the long lake and into Telos where they were sluiced into the cut that connected with the Penobscot.

The cable for this backwoods conveyor belt powered by a steam engine was 6,000 feet long, weighed fourteen tons, and was fitted with 4,800 bolts, which arrived improperly sized and had to be retooled by hand on site. Some of the material was brought by boat, and the rest hauled by draft animals across frozen lakes in winter. In six seasons of use during the first decade of the century, the tramway hauled 100 million board feet of timber. About seven decades after Stanton's visit, McPhee termed the site "an oxidized hole of commerce." Such is history. By the agency of time a useful machine becomes garbage and then revered artifact.

A brief walk on a well-worn path took us to one of the oddest sites I've ever seen. Imprisoned by dense second growth were two 100-ton old-fashioned locomotives, side by side, their wheels frozen with rust to the tracks. They were massive, out of scale, out of time, out of place. They burned a black and white photograph on my mind, an indelible image I can recall clearly today, years and hundreds of miles from the woods. The engines themselves are not particularly remarkable. It's their presence here that's amazing.

Huge hulks of metal, they sit timelessly like giant ersatz boulders dropped by a retreating industrial glacier.

These oil-fired steam engines belonged to the Eagle Lake and Umbazooksus Railroad, yet another contrivance to get Allagash logs to float past Bangor. It opened in 1926 and ran about a decade. The tracks traversed about thirteen miles from Eagle Lake to Umbazooksus, crossing Allagash Stream with a 1,800-foot trestle. The logs were then floated to the West Branch of the Penobscot via Chesuncook Lake. In an average week 6,500 cords of wood were transported.

The woods seemed strangely quiet considering that thousands of men worked around here in the 1920s. I imagined conversations and laughter, the rattle and hum of machines, thud of axes, and sizzle of frying bacon.

The locomotives have such a forceful presence that it almost seemed as if the forest itself was out of place. What were the engineer's thoughts, I wondered, that day the loggers cut their last cord and the train was left abandoned, to be vandalized by both man and nature? Did they feel remorse or good riddance after thousands of trips together? Time and progress were brought to a halt, victims of their own success when the surrounding forest was fully cut. Now trees grow again as the engines rust away.

Alice and I stood several minutes among the closely packed young trees, gaping at the great machines in silent fascination. Then, from far off it seemed, I heard the rustle of leaves. The wind! My body grew instantly rigid. Simultaneously we turned toward each other in dread and without a word ran back to the lake. A light breeze had begun rippling the water.

We quickly shoved off and paddled past Hog Island and the much larger Farm Island. Named in logging days, pigs were probably pastured on one and crops grown on the other. Light patches of birch and poplar, I'd read, indicated where clearings had once been made among the evergreens. A careful observer of landscape later instrumental in developing Michigan's mining industry, Hubbard saw much the same thing, observing that "years ago an incision was made and a budding farm ingrafted, but the wound has grown together again, and the scar is scarcely visible." Environmental healing is a long process.

A soft and pleasant breeze arose, bothersome to paddle against, but not particularly arduous. Alice suggested we have lunch at the Little Eagle campsite on a point of land at the far northern end of the lake. I wasn't hungry, and feared the wind might pick up at any moment. She insisted on having a bite to eat and needed to use the outhouse. I grumbled something under my breath and steered the boat toward shore.

Now I was the one hurrying to make more miles, perhaps as eager to be done with our partnership as to discover and explore what lay ahead. I was still smarting over her suspicions and resentment at my note-taking. It was an essential part of my trip, as strange as that might seem to her. More than that, it was an affront to the very spirit of the voyage, to the memory and methodology of Thoreau himself. The Concord naturalist, McPhee observed, "had in his pack some pencils and an oilskin pouch full of scratch paper—actually letters that customers had written to his family [pencil making] business, ordering plumbago and other printing supplies. On the backs of these discarded letters he made condensed, fragmentary, scarcely legible notes" that he later expanded in his journal. I imagined an exhausted Thoreau, hunched over his papers in the evening just as I was doing. It wasn't only the great man's wake I hungered to follow. I was sure no one hassled him about his daily scribbling.

Was McPhee, I wondered, also writing about his own technique? A brilliant essayist who quickly got to the very essence of both the obvious and mysterious, his people and places leapt off the page. How would my words ever achieve such vibrancy without the immediacy of flipping open a pad and jotting notes regardless of weather, happenstance, and the preferences of people around me?

I'd now even more come to emphatically realize that canoeing was not just a matter of coordinating paddle strokes. There were personal needs like rest and comfort stops, or just wanting to fish, write or explore. On a canoe trip you can't escape from your companion's conversation, dietary oddities, or bodily necessities so you resolve to just get used to them. One's idea of working together begins to encompass more than navigating, pitching a tent, and cooking. My impatience made me feel small and a little mean spirited. Anger simmered just beneath my voice. Either there develops the kind of mutual tolerance and respect that is the best of any serious partnership, or the trip fails. The jury was still out—on both the trip and the relationship.

Once on shore, I found that I, too, needed rest and some food. But there wasn't much time to relax. Within fifteen minutes the wind had risen to the point of driving whitecaps in the center of the lake. We hastily packed the gear and pushed off, rushing like a prairie farm family to the storm cellar in the face of a twister.

Rounding the point on which we lunched, we entered the Thoroughfare, a narrow river-like connection leading to Churchill Lake. It opened in the middle to form relatively small Round Pond. On the map, it looked like a blue snake with a freshly swallowed mouse or frog in its belly. Along the western shore were bright green lowlands, and all around drowned trees that were sun-bleached and contorted. The wind failed to follow us, and the quiet water echoed as a pileated woodpecker drummed loudly on a hollow tree, his red crest and black and white striped face reminding me of an African ceremonial mask. Two wary moose watched us carefully from the shallows, and the soft hooting of loons sounded eerily from behind.

While on the pond, we were overtaken by two boats of teenagers whose harsh Brooklynese carried loudly over the water. Their accents brought to mind the whoosh of traffic and the patter of soles on sidewalks. I recalled listening to my dad's Brighton Beach memories about heading to Coney Island for a five-cent hotdog at Nathan's and a ride on the Wonderwheel, or an afternoon in the cheap seats at Ebbets Field.

All four boys were repeatedly hooting in excellent imitation of a loon just ahead. Captivated by the "duck," they watched it dive, betting with each other on where it would next surface. Greeting us heartily as they passed, I overheard one of them asking another how we managed to keep a steady course without switching sides to paddle. If they were so canoe-innocent as to be unaware of the stern j-stroke, I hoped they weren't so foolhardy as to attempt the rough water of Chase Rapids below Churchill Dam. Regardless, a little sound of the city caused me to feel the woods more sharply, and I imagined them bringing a bit of the woods back with them to Flatbush or Crown Heights.

After passing under John's Bridge, a narrow road crossing whose pilings were boxed in with planks to protect them from ice, the sky suddenly turned gray and began to spit. It felt as if the weather was chasing us, driving us hard. Continuing our paddle through the Thoroughfare, we soon emerged on the broad expanse of Churchill Lake whose Indian name, Allagaskiwigamook—Bark Cabin Lake—was shortened and given to the Allagash River issuing from its north end. After the confines of the Thoroughfare, entering three-mile-long Churchill was startling even though the low lying hills surrounding it made it less dominating in its setting than Eagle or Chamberlain. To the north, a dramatic ridge made of wear-resistant igneous rock several-million years old rose steeply about 400 feet above the water.

Wind made a lumpy landscape of the lake, which is said to be over sixty feet deep, and we pushed on to camp at the north end only with considerable effort. Despite the heavy water, I couldn't keep my eyes off the densely wooded shore whose dark pointy evergreens seemed like rockets ready to launch into an armada of charcoal clouds. At Schofield Point, the first neck of land visible on entering the lake, we spotted several deer.

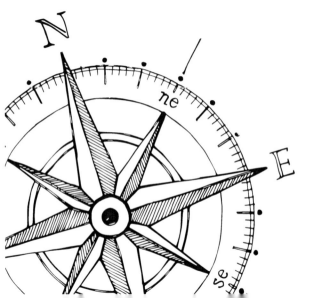

CHASE RAPIDS AND UMSASKIS

lice and I spent a lazy afternoon watching wind whip whitecaps on Churchill. Our campfire danced in the gusts. After sundown the breeze blew even harder, and in the morning we found our canoe flipped. Fortunately, we had the bowline tied to a tree. In the tent that evening, I had waited until I was certain Alice was asleep before hastily scribbling in my notepad under the cover of my sleeping bag. In the middle of the night, I awoke with pen still in hand.

While brooding over a lumpy gray sky, we ate a hearty breakfast of pancakes. Soon, patches of blue began playing hide-and-seek with the sun until a fair day erupted with giant, racing cumulous clouds. Just before nine o'clock, we launched the boat and paddled through the narrows that lead from Churchill to much smaller Heron Lake, once a holding pond for logs. Soon we beached at Churchill Dam. The river lay before us, starting with nine-mile-long Chase Rapids.

Only a couple buildings remain of the busy logging community that once thrived at Churchill Dam. In the 1940s, it had had enough children to have a schoolteacher by the name of Helen Hamlin who recorded her experiences in a book called *Nine Mile Bridge: Three Years in the Maine Woods*. She described the place as a "lumberjack colony . . . considered too wild and desolate for a woman teacher." But she spoke French at a time when most of the families were French Canadian, and had asked for a backwoods assignment. She found Churchill "a common-place looking settlement." Most of the homes "were identical, one-and-a-half-story company houses that had once been painted white." There were a few log cabins, henhouses, woodsheds, outhouses, garden plots and pigsties. She described the boardinghouse as "long, barracks-like."

On the west side an old bunkhouse still stands, and on the east there's a battered barn and ranger's cabin. It was here that the wealth of the forests was divided. Downstream of the dam, logs went north to the St. John. Upstream they were destined for the Penobscot and Bangor.

Hubbard, and later Stanton, found no dam. It had been dynamited by Canadian loggers eager to have more water in the Allagash to float their logs. Hubbard correctly prophesized that the time was "not too far distant when the tourist will see Chase Dam resurrected, and the forests now haunted by the moose will ring again with the choppers axe." Though the great pines had already been cut in his time, the massive spruce drives for pulpwood were yet to come.

Churchill Dam was rebuilt, but breached in 1958. A new timber-crib dam was built in 1968 upstream of the old one. During times when the dam was gone, one would have faced an unregulated flow, boisterous with high water early in the year, boney with rocks as summer wore on. Fortunately for the convenience of the paddling public, the existence of the dam allows release of sufficient water for canoes to float Chase Rapids in even the driest seasons.

Although not considered especially difficult in these days of virtually indestructible plastic laminate canoes like ours, Chase Rapids is the longest and most difficult stretch of whitewater on the Allagash. Old timers in the era of birch bark and canvas were much more respectful of the fast running river with its sharp ledges, souse holes and standing waves. One early twentieth century commentator maintained that guides earned their $4 per day, "for a city man fairly puts his life in their hands."

In the hallowed tradition of Allagash portage services, we had our gear trucked around the whitewater and dropped at the base of the rapids by the Churchill Dam ranger, whose cheerful dog greeted us first on our arrival. For a $10 fee we ran the canoe empty. Lightening the boat increased our maneuverability in the rough water, making the trip less dangerous and more fun. Standing by the dam and looking into the swirling, boiling downriver flow, we debated at length whether to have our gear portaged. The discussion was without the acrimony of our deliberation on Chamberlain Lake. We both walked on eggshells, fearing to attempt the fast moving water in a state of disharmony. To some enthusiasts, paddling sans baggage might seem a little like cheating, but knowing that many travelers have skipped the rapids altogether or allowed their guides to do the work made our approach seem a reasonable middle way.

It felt good to be back in the rush of fast water, see sunlight sparkle in the riffles and feel the current's power. Driven by the charging flow, we swung around tight bouldery curves and dodged through rock gardens. The river's hurry filled all sensation as it frothed and eddied around us. Not only did we experience quick cinematic views, we were engulfed in sound, watery smells and the feel of the river vibrating though the paddles.

Stanton ran Chase in a howling thunderstorm and with some hyperbole called it "the worst place run by canoemen in the state." Walled in by pointy spruces and overhanging cedars, we found ourselves sharing his experience.

> Towering banks, with dense jungle, are on both sides; immense trees lean over the stream as if to grab you. The current runs like a millrace; great boulders are everywhere,

alongside of you, under you, and you are lucky if some do not get on top of you. The channel, if there is one, is narrow and constantly circling around and among huge boulders, first on one side of the river and then on the other; in the middle and then where the onrushing waters take you. Canoes are constantly being swamped. Along the bottom of the river one catches glimpses of bakers, tin cans, kettles, bags of provisions—in fact, all kinds of camp equipage lost by unfortunate canoemen. Some day Chase's Carry will be worked to good advantage, as there is lots of pay dirt deposited there and more being constantly added.

Unlike our paddling till now, in Chase Rapids the world was altered every time we looked. Rocks and shore came up quickly. We turned to find a new angle of light glancing off the vegetation or reflecting from the water. At every bend, the height of the banks, tree silhouettes, and the water's movement around rocks contrived a new scene. Earlier we had absorbed the view like taking photographs; now we were making a movie.

Swapping the positions we'd held so far, Alice insisted on taking the stern in whitewater. She claimed to be the better judge of general navigation, finding the shifting channel and dodging obstacles. I wasn't so sure. Certainly, her eyesight was better, at least after my glasses were sprayed with water. Regardless, I agreed to man the bow where quick, decisive action was required for frequent, sudden course corrections.

Of course, the decision was about more than where we sat. In a canoe, the stern is the dominant and supervising position that steers the boat. Alice's desire to paddle stern was more than a strategic navigational adjustment and so was my assent. I had doubts, but this wasn't a time to argue.

If ever there is a situation in which two people must instinctually anticipate their partners' moves, it is in the surge of whitewater.

With no time for deliberation or argument, a missed signal can be fatal or result in serious injury even in a relatively mild reach like Chase. Success depends less on the skill of the partners, then on their ability to work together.

We sluiced through the stone-laden channel, sliding between and around large rocks, riding the main flow, charging through standing waves and banking curves. All the while we yelled and gestured instructions to each other over the pounding roar. Around a blind curve, we encountered a stretch dotted with rocks where water flowed in two distinct, but hard to read channels before rolling over hidden boulders. Our signals got crossed and suddenly the boat shuddered with a blow to the bow. In quick succession we banged against several rocks like a pinball hitting bumpers. The water's force pushed us sideways and in an instant we were wedged perpendicular to the flow.

With the water pinning us against the rocks like a powerful wrestler, we pushed with our paddles in every conceivable combination of force and at various angles but were unable to extricate ourselves. I was boiling angry. Why had I ever relented and let her paddle stern? In Alice's face I saw my own fury reflected. Having to yell to be heard over the water only provoked us further. Rage seemed to devour us, and soon we were perched in midstream screaming at each other.

In whitewater training, few instructors will let couples paddle together until they well understand river hydraulics and the stakes of making a mistake. After all, it's much easier to argue and get angry with an intimate than with a stranger. Perversely, we save our most savage conflicts for those we care about. In an effort that involves as much judgment and coordination as individual skill, your first inclination, however misguided, is to blame your partner for the miscalculation. Such instances telescope all the little annoyances and irritations of living in close quarters into a moment. Hard feelings erupt like a rash you cannot help but scratch despite knowing that scratching only makes things worse. You may realize you will regret everything you are saying, but remain helplessly caught in the swirling maelstrom of your own emotions.

Finally exhausting our anger, we were silent for a few seconds as the roaring river seemed to take up all the space around us. We had a common enemy, and since screaming at each other was not freeing us from the water's grip, we made hasty apologies. We both got out of the boat onto some stones, and after a minute of strenuous rocking and wrangling with the current, freed the canoe.

As we cascaded swiftly down river, it seemed like the planet itself had suddenly tilted in the direction we were going and I felt a little woozy, like a drunk negotiating a steep staircase. Suddenly we both erupted in laughter. Nothing was particularly funny, but release from the rocks was also an emotional release. We were louder than the water curling over ledges, paddling the last few drops so smoothly it seemed we were flying.

With the water's speed, the stress of constant lookout, and reflexive jabbing with our paddles to stay on course, Chase Rapids was by far the fastest nine miles of the trip, regardless of our time on the rocks. It left us almost as drained as had the wind on Chamberlain and Eagle. My legs wobbled like Jell-O when at last we stepped back on shore and fell into each other's arms with deep kisses. We easily found our gear where the ranger had left it at the end of a dusty road.

Once done with the all-consuming vigilance required in the rapids, the steady, slow float to Umsaskis Lake was relaxing. Tension seeped slowly out of us. Again we had the luxury of watching the tree-lined shore and following the madcap dives of regally crested kingfishers. The sun was bright and the river glistened as if inlaid with silver. Still, anger continued to pulse deep inside me. Emotional wounds had stopped bleeding, but still throbbed. I could tell by her aggressive silence that Alice felt the same.

Just before entering Umsaskis (Abanaki for lakes linked together), the thick evergreen forest yielded to a bright grassy meadow. In this "wide boggy low slung valley" the lanky essayist Hoagland spied red-winged blackbirds and bitterns. We saw Canada geese and heard loons yodel. Others have seen great blue herons, mergansers, muskrats, and black ducks.

Three miles long and over half a mile wide, Umsaskis is surrounded by lush, rolling green hills. The sky was large, with clouds that seemed brushed on, high and delicately feathered. Sunlight was warm and pure, a simple pleasure. We imbibed the landscape and grew inebriated in its glow. Chase Rapids' strain melted and seeped out of us as we stole reassuring glances at each other, our feelings of distrust and anger mellowing in the surrounding beauty.

The lake seemed to draw all that was around it to its center. Even the horizon appeared to dip in homage to the water as if the very axis of the planet turned on this spot. Here, in comprehensible size, the beauty of all Allagash lakes was concentrated.

We passed under a metal truss bridge carrying a logging road as we were leaving the lake. Shortly afterward, we camped on the western shore. In the warm afternoon sunshine, setting up camp was a chore to be savored. After a dinner of beef jerky, instant soup, and cheese, we fished, each of us catching ten-inch chubs. Offering even greater sport were the gnats we slapped at incessantly as they swarmed from the woods at twilight. Invariably, as I felt a tug on my line there was a no-see-um pinch on the back of my neck and I lost the fish in the distraction. No doubt these were all sixteen-inch brook trout.

Fortunately, September is not a bad month for the bugs that have caused such abject misery in spring and summer. In a generally dry, official geological report from the 1830s, Jackson reported that "dense swarms of black flies and mosquitoes almost disabled us in our labors." Thoreau went so far as to say on his second trip that the best nights were rainy because there were no bugs.

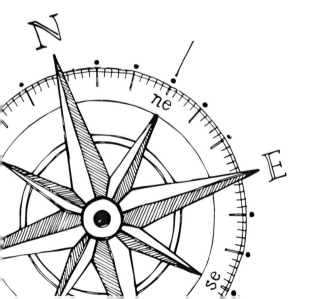

DOWNSTREAM TO SWEENEY BROOK

Morning was cool and showery so we took our time getting up for breakfast. Hungover from yesterday's squabble in the rapids, I awoke in a foul mood. Alice's was complementary. The night had been restless. I didn't sleep well with her throaty snoring and everything in the tent was damp and clammy. Fortunately, in my sleeplessness, I was rewarded with the sounds of echoing loons.

During most of the trip, we had felt hurried and inconvenienced by the weather. Between heat and humidity at the beginning, then wind, cold, rain and drizzle, it had been difficult to enjoy rest stops, linger to observe wildlife, or to fish, and almost impossible to take a decent lunch break. As we shivered over morning chores and a breakfast of instant oatmeal and dried fruit, our eyes glanced furtively at the sky, as if we were afraid of being overtaken in a desperate chase. Menacing clouds briefly spit and then suddenly stopped. We brooded like petulant children.

While Alice washed the breakfast dishes, I decided to consult the map to see where the river would take us. I found it lying limp and soggy on a stone in front of the fire ring. We had scrutinized it in the yellowish glow of a weak flashlight before lying down for the night. I'd assumed Alice had brought it into the tent since taking her turn as the last one out, she had hung the food bag in a tree, made sure the canoe was tied up, and the camp secure.

Simmering frustration over the weather came too quickly to a boil. I ran down to the riverbank where Alice was rinsing our coffee cups. With acid annoyance, I demanded to know why she'd left the map out overnight. Echoing my tone of voice, she threw the accusation back like a major league fastball. Since in my "obsession" with charting our progress, I'd brought the map out, she figured I would put it away.

There must have been a bit of flammable residue left from our shouting match in Chase Rapids. With frightening swiftness, the wet map blew up into a clash about breakfast chores, putting purification tablets in the water bottles, and the proper way to roll a sleeping bag. Although these matters might appear trivial at home, they loomed large here in the woods where such details were essential not only to comfort, but safety. Our bickering felt much like being in the grip of a violent rapid pulling us inexorably toward a boulder despite frantic efforts to back-paddle and steer around it.

I matched everything she said with a return accusation or a condescending reply—or perhaps she was matching me. At times I couldn't tell which was parry and which thrust. The argument seemed to have a life of its own as the substance of the encounter faded into a raging whirlpool of indignation and fury sucking us both down. In some calm recess of my mind, like a light filled draw in the dense spruce forest, I knew we were on a useless and destructive course, but I felt powerless against my own anger. With a resounding "fuck you" that was more than matched in volume and vitriol, I stalked up the bank, through the campsite and into the woods. Behind me I heard the metal dishes Alice was washing crash to the ground with considerable force.

Standing among the gloomy spruce, slowly dripping icy water like a gently squeezed sponge, was sobering. My ire quickly dissipated, leaving a residue of shame and regret. It somehow felt tangible, like an embarrassing physical deformity. In five minutes I was back at the campsite where Alice sat sullen and dejected. With a few carefully chosen words of apology and a hug more reflexive than friendly, we soon arrived at a tense truce. Given our position, what real choice was there? There was nowhere to go and brood about our feelings for any length of time. The trip itself forced us to work together, to cultivate confidence and comfort even. There was no other way.

Long after we were out of the woods, Alice told me that she had resolved at that point to leave me as soon as the trip was over, and would have done so immediately if we'd been at home. I felt the same. Every once in a while, there have been moments when I wondered if we would have been better off following through on our anger and exasperation and just breaking up. We could have agreed to a cease-fire lasting just long enough to get us out of the woods and away from each other for good.

At about 10:30 we were on the water with the wind almost directly behind. Despite a threatening sky, the rain held off. But good fortune didn't last long. Within twenty minutes a hard downpour began and continued for the better part of an hour as we paddled a five-mile-long finger of water known as Long Lake. Wind-driven drops plopped onto the surface like coins. Clouds trailed dark, ragged threads of precipitation. We were chilled and uncomfortable. The weather seemed to express our feelings, intensifying the sense of being handcuffed to one another.

As the rain let up, sheets of mist moved across the glowing green landscape and seemed to disappear into the grayness of the lake. Soon, lighter clouds and patches of blue worked their way into the sky. Strong winds and massive dirigible-like clouds came to dominate the day.

The hillside on the western shore of Harvey Pond, into which Long Lake empties, was beautifully pied with light and dark greens from a mix of hardwoods and conifers, apparent testimony to the farm which once stood there. It may have been Long Lake Farm. Here Stanton stopped to replenish his supply of sugar wetted in Chase Rapids.

At the end of Harvey Pond, we stopped at Long Lake Dam for lunch. Only the ruined dam—a jumble of rocks, soil, and timber— reminded us that this was not an absolutely wild place. It was hard envisioning the 700 foot-long structure with its fifteen-foot head of water. The rushing flow below the dam hid ledges that had been dynamited to ease the passage of boats and logs.

As we ate, I felt the forest close around us. The only sound was water. Suddenly I was struck at how the river and its lakes were now what they'd always been since the coming of humans—arteries of commerce, though now recreation, not Native hunting or logging was the business. I was grateful for the river's boisterous sound which filled the air and made less a necessity of conversation as we sullenly munched on chunks of salami, cheese and bread roughly cut with a Swiss Army knife.

I stared at the ragged skyline of trees, intricate, dendritic shapes that seemed as complex as music, and as hypnotic. It was a peaceful vista with the inevitable lone white pine standing above the surrounding forest like a ship's mast. For some reason, these singular evergreens had been spared by loggers. Perhaps some defect left them not worth cutting.

Allagash logging occurred in two stages. In the early days, only pines were considered worthwhile timber. They were felled mostly in the mid to late nineteenth century for use as saw logs. Trees of "somber grandeur," as historian Lew Dietz put it, some were six feet in diameter at the butt and 150 feet tall. So large were the stumps, that it was said that a man who cut such a tree would never live to see what was left in the ground rot away.

Pines grew as islands in the dense spruce forest, usually clustered along river banks where they were easily harvested and floated to market. Timber cruisers would climb high into trees or to hill-tops and map the veins of pine. Some boasted they could plot the course of a river by where the pines stood. Thoreau imagined these lumber explorers "a hundred miles or more from any town, roaming about and sleeping on the ground where night overtakes them." He wished, he wrote, "that I was with them."

It was more like mining than harvesting. After all, "harvesting" suggests a renewable supply. It could take hundreds of years to produce such trees, which Stanton wrote, "seemed to have lived in the age of human giants and the animals and fish of biblical times."

After the woods were practically stripped of pines, spruce was cut for papermaking pulpwood. These trees stood in thick formations and could be felled on a grand scale. The pulpwood age replaced the axe with the saw and gave birth to mechanical contraptions, the remains of which rust away at the tramway site on Eagle Lake and elsewhere. Although the pine era was romantic, Dietz notes, it was pulping with its expensive capital investments that started lumbermen thinking about the future and the need to grow as well as cut trees. Pulpwood harvesting continues today just beyond the curtain of vegetation that forms the official state owned boundary of the Allagash Wilderness Waterway.

Travelers in these woods have always felt ambiguity about logging. In sympathy with Thoreau, we sometimes decry the forest's destruction and the use of money as the only way to value a tree. Yet, we prize books, furniture, houses, and other products the wood provides. Furthermore, like Thoreau, we are fascinated by lumbermen, often idealizing and sentimentalizing their rough elemental ways. The complete story includes such notions, but is a complex economic web hidden from those with overly romantic views that prevent them from seeing the forest for the trees. It includes profit hungry capital from distant cities, environmental damage, brutally hard work, and families fed with the fruits of the forest.

Occasionally, Alice and I heard the grinding whine of chain saws or the rumble of skidders. Once we saw a fully loaded log truck crossing a narrow bridge over the river. It was annoying, intrusive, and distracting—a dose of something I had come to avoid. Were the pristine-looking trees deceptive, like old time Hollywood backdrops? Although the state-owned a 500-foot beauty strip and regulated timbering on private land a mile back from the water, it sometimes seemed a bureaucratic sleight of hand. Perhaps it was the best that could be expected in an era of burgeoning populations demanding a variety of wood products from newspapers to toothpicks.

Of course, canoeists no longer see decaying camps and woodsmen sorting logs like travelers did at the turn of the century. Ironically, it was the large-scale ownership patterns necessitated by industrial logging that to some extent preserved a broad landscape in Allagash country and kept it from being hopelessly broken up into small parcels.

Today's reality is a place neither solely consigned to timbering or wilderness, but the locus of a tug-of-war between rival human desires. For over 150 years this tension has been an Allagash hallmark, and testimony to the river's resiliency. Although a wilderness appears around you, signs of logging ensure this is no truly remote place or Disney fantasy. Our fascination toward the tramway site and other vestiges of logging suggest that equivocation over the intrusions of civilization has long been part of the Allagash experience.

Horseboats were a colorful feature of the spruce era in the late nineteenth and early-twentieth centuries. Long Lake Dam, where we now found ourselves, was a major terminal for these vessels. Flat bottom boats, about forty feet long and twelve to fourteen feet in the beam, were drawn in the river by two wading horses who occasionally had to swim. A long sweep in the stern was used to steer. The boats brought supplies to upstream lumber camps.

The vessels took half a day to reach Allagash Falls from their start in Allagash Village at the confluence with the St. John River. From here, gear would be portaged and loaded on a second boat above the falls. Another three days were required to reach Long Lake Dam. Ninety years ago, a traveler might have encountered one of these boats just below the dam. Imagine a crew of French-Canadian's togged out in gray knee socks, knickers and red mackinaws. Two men in the bow would be poling on each side to keep the ungainly craft off the rocks while, perched on top of the cabin's slanting roof, the skipper steered with the long sweep oar.

We launched our canoe into a constricted channel that increased the current and hurried us over the remains of Long Lake Dam, a rock and timber structure built by the St. John Lumber Company in 1907. It had boasted eighteen gates. The water impounded was said to extend the spring log drive by ten days. It seemed amazing that such a grand structure could be reduced to rubble in just a few decades.

Once passing over the old dam, the river became placid. We paddled another couple miles, passing to the left of Cunliffe Island and camping at Sweeney Brook. Despite wilderness designation, place names along the river still memorialize logging days. A tough, tight fisted and mean man, Will Cunliffe operated a large logging company. A logger who left the woods for church one Sunday, river historian Dietz writes, was asked what penance the priest had prescribed. "Go into the woods and work for Will Cunliffe," was the mischievous reply.

John Sweeney, whose name was given to the brook near where we camped, was a logging boss. It's said that he once blew up Lock Dam on Chamberlain Lake in order to get logs flowing north in accordance with the water's natural course.

After pitching the tent and cooking a dinner of noodles topped with canned sauce and slices of pepperoni, we sat at the river's edge and watched the forest grow gradually darker. We hadn't seen another person all day and the woods around us seemed dense and ominous. As twilight came and the wind died, a crescent moon rose and the last rays of sunlight focused on a glowing rim of horizon. There was just enough light to cast a rough-edged reflection on the water where spruce, birch, pine, and cedar lined the bank. Rocks hidden just below the riffled surface seemed to wobble in the mirrored image. Alice and I still had little to say to each other and our camp chores were performed mechanically. My focus shifted to our surroundings.

A queer feeling overtook me that evening, as if we had paddled back in time. It seemed as if this place had remained unchanged since before the first pilgrim set foot on Plymouth Rock. Like Indians of old, we had begun to measure distance by a day's paddle. Something of this country was seeping inside me. Despite the tension between Alice and me, I felt helplessly and delightfully enchanted with my surroundings. Merely paddling seemed an act of naked possession. I felt an ownership interest of sorts, a usufruct right granting a power greater than any deed filed on the land records. Perhaps I'd been touched by the omnipresent Indian spirit, Manitou. This fundamental life force of the Algonquain people was found in natural phenomena like animals, plants, and landscape features. Certainly, I'd been enraptured by the loon, messenger of Glooskap, the world's creator according to Native legend. Indian culture may have been diminished by the onslaught of civilization, but fragments of Indian sensibility, it seemed, might yet take possession of a person opening himself to this land.

ROUND POND, MUSQUACOOK
DEADWATER, CUNLIFFE DEPOT

It was cold at six in the morning. The sun was taking its time rising over a tall picket of trees lining the river. Mist wafted across the water and my hands reddened, stiffened as Alice and I engaged in the usual camp chores. Despite the blowups of recent days, we still could work well with each other. Affections were strained, but our ability to take care of the mechanical business of living seemed strangely little affected. It gave me hope that we might recover our equilibrium and overcome the downward spiral that the stress of the trip seemed to foment.

Soon after launching, we came upon a cow moose feeding in the riffles, a dreamy apparition in billowing fog. Afterwards, imaginary moose appeared in every dark boulder and partially submerged log lurking in shadowy light. Around the next bend, mergansers and Canada geese swam as effortlessly as if it were fog and not water on which they glided. U. S. Supreme Court Justice William O. Douglas considered early morning haze the "finest hour" on the Allagash. "Details are distorted," he wrote, "until prosaic promontories—even colorless down logs—take on bizarre forms."

Soon we found ourselves on the river's second and larger Round Pond, quiet and insular in its hills, separated from the other lakes by a long stretch of river. On the east shore was Windy Point, a narrow peninsula hosting Jalbert's Sporting Camps, built in the 1940s by Willard Jalbert, Sr. and his two sons. It was the senior Jalbert, known affectionately as "The Old Guide," who took Justice Douglas down river, telling tales of the old ways and spicing the conversation with French-Canadian dialect.

A civil libertarian and vigorous outdoorsman, Douglas served a record over 36 years on the court. During that time he wrote more opinions and dissents than any other justice in history. In the landmark 1972 environmental case of *Sierra Club v. Morton*, he famously argued in dissent that inanimate natural resources like alpine meadows, beaches, and groves of trees ought to have standing to sue in court to prevent their despoliation. A river, he wrote, in his opinion, perhaps thinking of his time on the Allagash, is "the living symbol of all life it sustains or nourishes . . . . The river as plaintiff speaks for the ecological unit of life that is part of it."

Over a dozen years before penning those words, Douglas had come to Maine to be the voice of the river and advocate for its protection. He argued for dam removal and a wide corridor "free of roads, free of resorts, free of all marks of civilization." Calling a future restored Allagash "the most wondrous canoe stream in the nation," he maintained that a person experiencing its marvels "would give his own life before he saw them destroyed."

We saw a few fishermen trying their luck on the pond in water so dark and still it looked almost solid. Paddling north, we again entered the river and rode through the crackle and pop of Round Pond Rips, a short and gentle stretch of quickwater. By piers of a washed-out bridge, we stopped and caught five chub on shiny spoon lures. We kept four of them for dinner. The day grew bright and warm.

After the rips, we passed Turk Island where a draft horse of that name fell into a deep hole and drowned while pulling a boat. Bending eastward, the river slowed and darkened again. Banks became steeper, the countryside hillier. One hill sported a broad band of bright green hardwoods where a generation ago a tornado had shaved a line in the woods south to Round Pond. After all these years you might have thought the scar no longer visible, but many travelers have mentioned it. A change in vegetation may be a memorial, constitute landscape memory.

Further downstream where Musquacook (Abanaki for Muskrat place) Stream pours silently into the Allagash, we entered another slow and deep reach, five-mile long Musquacook Deadwater. Riffles and rocks disappeared in the dark, waxy flow, and plants, leaning gently downstream, grew in shallows. Resting on our packs in warm sun, we let the slight current carry us.

Without wind or rushing water, our normal conversational voices seemed loud, filling the space around us. Turning toward one another we floated slowly, enjoying the gaze of a dirty, but familiar face as if we were drifting on a rubber raft at some weekend resort. Perhaps it was the luxurious ease with which we moved, but I felt myself softening toward Alice. There'd still been no real resolution or apology to repair our damaged relationship, just passage of time and territory. It felt like a thunderstorm had raged and then passed. I'd resigned myself to surreptitious note-taking at odd moments and late at night.

On a chilly autumn day, the intrepid Lucius Hubbard, lawyer and later geologist, along with his very hungry party reached this section of the Allagash after leaving at Churchill Lake and traveling a hard, seldom used route with tough portages that took them by way of the Musquacook chain of lakes and Musquacook Stream. Arriving at noon, they lunched on their last beaver tail, a can of tomatoes, and soup powder. A keen observer of nature and lover of remote and mysterious places who liked making due with the materials at hand, it's little wonder that he later became a collector of *Gulliver's Travels* and *Robinson Crusoe* books.

Hubbard found the country around the river unattractive and

burnt, charred trunks contrasting with a foot of fresh snow. The scorching from the previous season was caused by two hunters careless with fire. Today the forest is thick, broken by occasional riverside meadows and hemmed in with vegetated hills.

As we left Musquacook Deadwater we came upon a young, scraggly bearded guide who had just helped his hefty sport to a fifteen-inch trout. He scoffed at our chub. Then, as if feeling sorry for our misfortune, he directed us in confidential tones to an over-grown path in the woods leading to an old and severely dilapidated log cabin. It lacked windows and had a decided lean, but its most remarkable feature was a living roof. Hand cut cedar shakes covered with birch bark appeared watertight despite roughly an inch of soft green moss and several small trees growing on it. Even the light here was green; the air smelled of moist earth. The cabin seemed to have sprung out of damp soil like a mushroom. A man-built structure that appeared to have made its peace with the woods, the cabin seemed emblematic of humanity's long-standing give and take with this region.

Grateful to have been alerted to the cabin, we nevertheless hadn't appreciated the guide's dissertation on the unique suitability of chub as bait. Such mixed feelings about guides are an Allagash tradition, and perhaps a primary reason why in this do-it-your-self age they are seldom employed by paddlers. In the nineteenth century, by contrast, Native American guides were all the rage. But although admired for their knowledge of woods lore and ability to handle a birch in rough water, complaints about guides were legion, some principals raging about their unreliability and deceitfulness.

Regardless of the attitude of their employers, guides did the bulk of the work, taking the canoe through tricky rapids, carrying large portage loads, and cooking the inevitable three Bs—bread, bacon and boiled potatoes. One nineteenth century sportsman even got his Indian guides to blow up a couple of air mattresses by suggesting a contest between them. He saw great sport in watching the two compete and, of course, pronounced the outcome a tie.

Unfortunately, one learns more about prevailing employer prejudices than about individual guides in nineteenth century accounts. In most cases, they are two dimensional figures, much like draft animals. Although Thoreau wrote more sympathetically about his guides than the others, he seems so locked into his preconceived notion of primitive culture that he largely fails to grasp the essence of these complex men. Oddly, this myopia contrasts with his general hunger for knowledge about Native languages, place names and craft techniques for which he clearly had great respect.

Joe Attien, Thoreau's 1853 guide, was a young, illiterate lumberjack famous as a riverman, an aristocrat of the Penobscot tribe, and son of a tribal governor. He disappointed Thoreau by whistling "O Susanna," using Yankee phrases like "By George!," and with his less than comprehensive knowledge of traditional skills. Joe Polis, his 1857 guide, was well acquainted with woodcraft, Indian vocabulary, and natural phenomena. He is more vividly rendered. But Thoreau misses the full depth of this educated Penobscot caught between cultures, a tribal leader and property owner who represented his people before the state and in Washington. He'd been to Boston, New York, Philadelphia, and other places, but understood cultural limitations. "I suppose, I live in New York, I be poorest hunter, I expect," Polis said.

As I learned more about, and worked with Native Americans as part of my job in Connecticut state government analyzing legal and historical Indian issues for legislators, I developed a deep regard for the daily struggles of Native peoples to retain their identity while living in the modern world. With Attien and Polis, Thoreau found the very fulcrum of the matter, but seemed to have missed the balance point.

In the later part of the twentieth century, Edward Hoagland painted one of the most sensitive pictures of a guide. Fred King was an experienced Maine woods denizen who had been a shipyard pipefitter in World War II. As if he were sketching a heartfelt character for one of his novels, Hoagland took an interest in King's background, empathized with his solitariness, and captured his speech rhythms. With small details, a multi-dimensional character emerged. King, Hoagland wrote, kept a jug of Allagash water at his Augusta home for mixing drinks. "So late we get smart," King would say, "so soon we get old."

Hoagland claimed he took the unfashionable measure of hiring a guide so as to allow time to write. But King was also a foil, full of information, a vivid personality who made the trip and the writing more interesting. Yet Hoagland, too, maintained equivocal feelings, regretting the noise of the motor and the chatty King who frightened animals. He found some solace in the suspect notion that "silence on the water was more Sierra Club nonsense," since old timers, he believed, made noise to dispel loneliness and chase away bears and panthers. I'm not sure what "old timers" he had in mind, since be they hunters or observers, travelers on the Allagash have always worked hard to see wildlife.

King was immortalized with a campsite in his name established on the northwest end of Eagle Lake. He was a roguish and independent sort who didn't care much for government regulations or private landowners' rules. Among other things, he established campsites without permission. The one on Eagle was finally made official in order to placate King. He was "a trickster full of tall tales," Dorothy Kidney described him while Alice and I warmed up in the cottage at Lock Dam.

Not far below the moss roofed cabin, we camped on the site of an old logging supply area once run by the imperious Will Cunliffe and known as Cunliffe Depot. We cleaned and fried the chub, which turned out to be delicious despite the guide's highbrow trout preferences. After dinner, we wandered out of the large clearing in which our tent was pitched and looked for firewood. Among the sticks and small branches we gathered, we found artifacts of logging days in the form of old bottles and cans, rusted machine parts and pieces of unclassifiable junk. A short path just upstream from our tent took us to two derelict Lombard Log Haulers, the earliest useable track-driven vehicle. First patented in 1901, the technology proved valuable for military tanks and bulldozers.

The old time loggers are not easily forgotten. They were physical men with reputations for swelled pride and hair-trigger tempers. Perhaps their legends will outlive even the rusting evidence of their presence still scattered about the woods. Certainly, the fight between Cut Chaise and Pierre Charette, both of whom worked on one of Cunliffe's last drives, are among the epic stories that will keep the larger-than-life stereotypes alive for generations.

After much acrimony between the two men, Chaise won the seemingly inevitable battle between them, but at the expense of his right ear. "Pierre, who had chewed it off," Dietz writes, "averred a bit sullenly that even with salt Cut Chaise's ear would have been no delicacy." My disagreements with Alice seemed relatively mild in comparison. This quiet riverside field was once a rough and tumble place.

Perhaps it was the fair weather, the novelty and mystery of the cabin, the time we spent fishing, or simply the enforced rhythm and coordination of our paddling, but the painful quarrel over the map seemed distant, a vaguely remembered hurt. We'd spent practically every second since then in close company, and by common effort put many miles between us and the site of our altercation. The thread of hard feeling seemed to fray, became awkwardly woven into the fabric of the adventure and our relationship.

As the cool evening fell around us like a thick blanket, we drew close together and settled in front of a fire that rippled and flowed like the river's current. Ensconced in the broad field, the dome of the sky pierced with points of white, cold starlight seemed incomprehensively large. In the emptiness of night, I held Alice closely, and she snuggled her head into my chest.

It seemed as if we were the only people for miles around, and indeed it was likely we were. Yet, I felt a presence. Perhaps it was the spirit of the old-time loggers or the long-gone travelers whose writings drew me here. The woods were luminous with their words. But beyond such thoughts, I felt a spiritual presence in the forest and waters themselves. It had overtaken me as days passed. The feeling warmed me even in the cold, like a hot meal, satisfying and nutritious. "I believed that the woods were not tenantless, but choke-full of honest spirits as good as myself any day," Thoreau wrote while camping on Moosehead Lake in 1857, perhaps in a mood similar to mine. He found his surroundings "not an empty chamber, in which chemistry was left to work alone, but an inhabited house" in which he enjoyed fellowship.

We awakened around five o'clock the next morning to loud grunting, groaning and crashing. Images of wolves, bears, or at the very least coyotes gave me chills. Peering cautiously from the tent into the cold dark, I spotted an even greater nemesis—a rotund, thick-furred, masked bandit of a raccoon reaching for our garbage hung not quite three feet off the ground for lack of tall nearby trees. We made all sorts of bizarre noise and pointed our flashlights at the creature like laser guns to no avail. He might hesitate a second, but the raccoon seemed an experienced thief that no humans wrapped in a nylon cocoon were going to deter from his work. The ridiculousness of our attempts and the animal's indifference sent us into a breathless laughing jag, which also failed to disturb him. The raccoon retreated only with the rising sun.

ALLAGASH FALLS

ist was lifting off the water in thick clouds on an icy morning. As we paddled, the river grew shallower and wider, sporting islands that diverted the current into many channels. Silver maples became common, rustling in the wind, their light undersides catching the morning sun like old coins. Rolling green hills appeared in the distance and an ever widening margin of flat land bordered the river. Occasional waterlogged stumps, Hoagland thought, were moose shaped. Like Alice and I, he saw the river as "a dream—rustling, windy, wild looking, and lush—chipper with birds, overhung with sweepers, dense with slow channels forking between the islands."

In the late nineteenth and early twentieth centuries there were several farms between what was to become Cunliffe Depot and Allagash Falls. They supplied logging camps with fruits, vegetables and meats. Except for the ranger station at a place still called Michaud Farm just below Cunliffe, one would never know there had been any domestic or agricultural existence here. One farm was near a marshy area called Finley Bogan, a designation joining the name of farmer Finley McLellan with an Algonquian-based term meaning "stopping place." Indeed, back in the day these were often welcome rest stops for weary canoeists who could find provisions, a hot meal, and a night indoors. But the farmers were long gone and we were greeted by two great blue herons and a bittern as we passed among a series of goodly islands.

Going lazily downstream in easy current left ample time for banter. Our experiences in nature and humorous tales about our families led to sweet reminiscences and laughter. It filled time and relieved some of the pressure building along the fault lines of our relationship. Since we could always lapse back into paddling or landscape gazing, talk never felt forced or stilted. It was a natural outgrowth of the day's labors. Still, there was much unsaid, hurt feelings unresolved.

Talking in a canoe is not the simplest or smoothest activity. Especially on a breezy day, you must speak up to be heard over wind and water. You might as well be calling long distance on a static connection with body language and facial expressions all but invisible. If you're in the bow, you often suffer the annoyance of having to turn around to be understood. Frequently, you miss something your partner utters, or are forced to repeat yourself. Just being confined with one person for long periods can be grating even if that person is saintly, but the added friction of difficult dialog sometimes erupts into temperamental skirmishes, a kind of emotional gorilla warfare. This morning was spiced with a few such misunderstandings which, fortunately, were quickly forgotten. Still, the difficulties of canoe conversation made it too easy to blame circumstance and avoid the real issues that lingered perilously between us.

I've yet to unravel the paradox of being free in the wide outdoors with the sense of being closely confined, almost tied to another individual. Getting along with a partner under these conditions is quite remarkable when you can barely stand your own smell, let alone someone else's. Maybe our arguments weren't so unusual. After all, we could work together just like anyone else despite our disagreements and occasional disagreeableness.

Approaching the forty-foot drop at Allagash Falls, the river grows deep and rocky, darkly colored, and the shore densely is wooded. We worried because the breeze made it difficult to discern the warning sound of water crashing over the rocks ahead. About five minutes before sighting the portage trail, we heard an undercurrent among the rustling trees, a deeper, constant rushing like a heavy, steady wind. By the time we landed, all our thoughts had been swallowed by the water's roar. The sound of the falls penetrates everything in the immediate area. We were constantly reminded of where we were.

The Maine geological survey of the 1830s found the area around Allagash Falls burned over with rough slate ledges poking above the soil. It may have been a bleak prospect for the scientists, but one that might have amplified the magnificent power of the falling water. Years later, hunter and fisherman Stanton enjoyed the benefits of fires in the taste of red raspberries growing in the scorched soil. The fruit also caused a bit of excitement. While an Indian guide was cleaning fish, a fair-sized bear was also enjoying the berries. The guide shot and wounded the animal with his lone cartridge. Hand-to-paw combat ensued, and when the rest of the group arrived on scene all they had was a knife. Breathlessly, they watched the Indian wrestle the enraged creature. The bear was soon dead and the Indian's arms "fearfully lacerated."

No bears disturbed our labors as we landed just above the falls. We hauled the first load of gear down the wide and worn carry trail, charging water echoing in our ears. Alongside the path, we passed an iron ring drilled into the rock. It had been used in horse-boat days to aid in hauling supplies with ropes. Our equipment and vessel moved over the very trail that had served as a primary freight artery for a major industry.

By the time we reached the carry's end at the base of the falls, I could feel the force of rushing water pounding in my chest. I looked toward Alice and found she was already gazing at me. In her hazel eyes I saw my own emotions reflected. In thrall to the water's hypnotic force, I felt pulled toward her. Perhaps it was the potency of falling water or the bond forced by the exhilaration of hard joint effort. Surrounded by the roar of the falls, we embraced long and tightly.

I became mesmerized by the constant roll and sparkle of falling liquid. Body and mind filled with the water's presence as if there were some mysterious force behind the glistening veil. It took a deliberate effort of will to be released. Only then did I clearly see the physical reality of this wide moving wall of water sliced in two by sharp ledges and foaming like detergent.

The same water against whose waves we struggled on the lakes and whose current lured us near dangerous obstacles on the river now roared with full animal strength. It had floated us, followed us, and surged ahead. Hot and fatigued from the portage, I took a long swig of Allagash water from my canteen and splashed my sweaty face.

A "fat, plentiful falls not notably high" the urbane New Yorker and world traveler Hoagland observed, the churning water spouting off rocks reminding him of a ship's wake. But even this skeptical, Harvard educated writer was moved by what he saw, surprised himself with an outpouring of emotion. "Looking down from above at the charade of destruction," he wrote, "suddenly I missed my wife. It was so lonely watching the water go over and smash that the mosquitoes began to seem friends." Something in the energy of this place causes a rush of sentiment.

Maybe it's the water's entrancing movement, or the solitude enforced by its roar, but Allagash Falls makes you stop, think, and consider yourself and the world. For hours afterward, my thoughts drifted in and out of the woods and I indulged in a self-Socratic dialogue. I wondered about my job, weighed relationships with my parents and friends, contemplated the drift of my life. Suddenly before me were the ambitions, doubts, and hopes usually reserved for the most quiet, private moments. I thought about a future with

Alice. We seemed to work well together, but not without tedious and sometimes explosive friction. I mostly enjoyed her company, but was I being fooled by the refreshing novelty of new vistas, fresh discoveries?

Perhaps simple, regimented travel by canoe and the knowledge that we would soon be returning home focused such thoughts. Yet, there was something special about this falls, a boiling reagent precipitating meditation. Whenever my feelings are overwhelmed or confused, I struggle to recapture these moments of lucidity when life's alternatives either seemed neatly mapped and navigable, or at least manageable. Maybe it's places like Allagash Falls that have stirred poets and philosophers with nature's coveted inspiration. Of course, introspection, poetry, and philosophy are not the only dreams born at this site. One guide thought Allagash Falls an excellent place for a pulp mill.

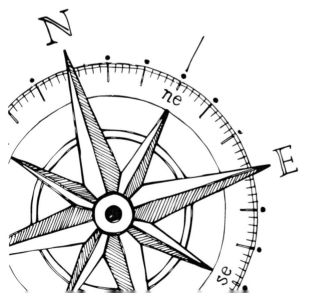

ALLAGASH VILLAGE

Stanton reached Allagash Falls when a log drive failed to get properly through. Logs were scattered along the shore from Round Pond to the St. John. Below the falls, the river was choked with pulpwood except for a narrow channel wide enough to maneuver a canoe. His party camped at the falls, though I can't imagine sleeping beside that freight train of sound. I surmise they didn't sleep well since around midnight they heard a noise like a baby crying. It returned whenever the wind blew away the watery roar.

The sound continued all night and at daybreak they investigated, finding a faun caught in the river between two logs. The doe was nowhere in sight so they picked up the baby, dried it off and fed it condensed milk and water. Taking it on as a passenger, they stopped at a farmhouse downstream and procured some cow's milk and a rubber nipple. Eventually they gave the faun away.

Where in Stanton's time about eighty years ago a canoeist would have witnessed the pulse of commerce, passing horse-drawn flatboats loaded with supplies, we saw only the river and trees. We paddled leisurely, not seeing a soul, stopping to fish now and again and reeling in a twelve-inch chub. Moving through fast water at McGargle Rocks, the sun sparkled in riffles of reflected light. Here a luckless Allagash logger drowned trying with his pike pole to pick a jam. We were carried swiftly along and soon McGargle was again forgotten.

A landscape of light green hills wound around the river. The prospect upstream had been much different with its tighter valley and boreal twilight of thick forest. We passed Ghost Bar Landing, a gravelly shoal near where a great pine crushed a logger. With a rotten heart, the tree was considered useless and left to decay beside the river. For years afterward, woodsmen reported seeing a ghost. It was said that the logger could not rest until the log he cut was floated. We saw no phantom on this pleasant day, and had hardly a thought of the brute effort and danger that once went into working on the Allagash. The river was crowded with history, though we saw not a soul.

Twin Brook Rapids is a rollercoaster of whitewater with frothy standing waves and a current split by rocks. In this onslaught of rough water and movement, Stanton felt his "heart and Adam's apple were holding close communion." After the difficult channels and shifting current of Chase Rapids, we negotiated the turbulence easily, navigating almost by instinct.

Although it's still six miles to the Village of Allagash at the river's confluence with the St. John, the rapids mark the end of the official "Wilderness Waterway." It's a political boundary determined by how far upstream the Dickey-Lincoln flood control and hydroelectric dam projects may drown the river and turn it into yet another linear lake. Dam building didn't end with the log drives, the projects just got more grandiose and found new purposes. For the time being, the lower Allagash flows unfettered. Though these dams now languish on the drawing board, their possible revival requires unblinking vigilance.

After passing Twin Brook Rapids, we heard trucks rumble along a road paralleling the river. The Allagash is a fragile area, perhaps more so politically than ecologically. Unlike the million plus acres of public property that insulates the canoe routes of the voyageur fur traders in northern Minnesota and adjacent Canada, this linear wilderness, and its thin, almost transparent curtain of trees that separates travelers on the river from the sight of skidders and large trucks, wasn't enough to keep a visitor from occasionally wincing at the sound of chainsaws. Now there wasn't even the official waterway's flimsy barrier we'd enjoyed upstream.

I don't know if the Allagash is a wilderness despite the high-minded language of the law creating the waterway. I do know that this place is isolated enough for a person to spend several days traveling outdoors surrendering their usual routine for something more nomadic, elemental, and closer to the earth. There comes a time in a trip such as this, McPhee observed, "when patterns that have been left behind fade beneath the immediacies of wind, sun, rain, fire, and a different sense of distance, of shelter, of food." Wilderness to some extent may be more a state of mind, a sensitivity of perception and willingness to see. In this respect, perhaps, I had more wilderness than those early timber cruisers seeking veins of pine in the virgin forest.

It might be that places placating human needs for beauty and primitiveness, retained at least in some areas, are as crucial to our survival as the need to exploit nature for jobs and products. This may be true even if those "wild" areas are not trackless, uninhabited regions. "In wildness," not *wilderness*, wrote Thoreau in his seminal essay "Walking," "is the preservation of the world."

Maybe with more land and a few hundred years this could again become a true wilderness. For now, it's still the backwoods, and the backwoods of Maine have always held their own particular pull and power as a place that is wild, if not wilderness.

Sometimes, we think we are left with a recently impoverished wilderness. In the 1880s, however, Steele's contingent was so overjoyed at seeing even the skull of a long dead moose that they extracted its teeth "fearing they would be the only souvenirs we should obtain of that almost extinct animal." We have lost the caribou, the wolf, wolverine and others, but in the backwoods of Maine moose now abound.

Achieving some semblance of solitude at times requires a trip out of synch with those starting down the river the same day, yet not catching up with those already on the water. But such problems were sometimes worse over a century ago. Hubbard found Eagle Lake with so many hunters that a person hardly dared fire a rifle for fear of hitting his neighbor. At night, the lake gleamed with campfires.

The wind whipped water on Chamberlain Lake a few days earlier was dangerously rough. Though we felt a bit cheated of a wilderness experience on landing ashore and discovering that a ranger in a power boat was poised to make a rescue if necessary, there was also some relief in knowing that should we have capsized, we need not have drowned. Afterward, I wondered if the rangers functioned somewhat like the settlers and loggers of earlier days who portaged, fed, housed, and otherwise aided travelers.

Perhaps it is the method of the canoe that most ties us to wilderness. By using this cigar-shaped vessel, regardless of high-tech materials, we travel back into an ancient realm of experiencing the world. Its rhythm, maneuverability, and limitations make this trip much of what it has always been since Indian times. A canoe trip is an act of communion with a place, a voyage taken not of necessity to get somewhere, but for the reward of the labor itself. Of course, a canoe remains the only practical means to penetrate the deep woods with all five senses free and on high alert. It creates a oneness with the river, lakes, and woods. This unity with nature is no doubt among the Indian virtues we most covet.

Following Twin Brook Rapids, the river becomes a bit tricky, running wide and shallow. It's easy to be lulled by a reach of fairly deep water and suddenly find yourself dead ended in shallows and shoals with no alternative but to retrace your path or carry the boat over a gravel bar.

In the chilly breezes of late afternoon we repeatedly scraped bottom, became stuck, and got out to pull the boat while following the water from one side of the river to the other in an attempt to take the deepest channel. With cold wind knifing through my jacket and constant frustration from running aground and struggling over sandbars to get afloat, I could feel the barely healed and tense anger at Alice crawling slowly up my back. Alice wore every bit of clothing she brought plus a sweater of mine. Still cold, I heard her curse under her breath. Ultimately, we turned most of the pressure outward and raged against the obstacles like tag-team wrestlers. In all the fury of getting the boat through, there was also joy in incremental progress.

The sky was exceedingly high, with fleecy cumulous clouds moving steadily. The wind seemed to draw cold off the water, stiffening our bodies as we struggled to keep warm. The road alongside the river grew busier, preparing us for civilization. Our last whitewater was fairly mild, and we made it through Eliza Hole Rapids with little effort. Here a work horse called Eliza drowned during a log drive. Finally, we hit Casey Rapids, named for an early area family, and situated at a sharp bend just before the confluence with the St. John.

We camped in an open field at Allagash Village where State Route 161 crosses near the river's mouth. Early in this century, the spot was described as having "hills as high as the highlands of the Hudson and as yet unmarred . . . there are beautiful cloud effects and charming vistas." It is still so.

The village is a faded cluster of homes with their backs against the woods. Logging trucks seemed more common than cars. Mc-Brierty's store had the lone set of gas pumps in town and the only public telephone, which also served as the store's business line. I went to make a call to arrange our pickup by floatplane downstream on the St. John the next day. Locals came and went for loaves of bread, canned goods, and cigarettes while a sour-faced woman presided from an old milk can serving as a stool. The top of the can was well polished from years of sitting.

Having been in the woods over a week, the rumble of cars, slam of the store door, and the act of dialing a phone seemed a little strange, like something remembered out of childhood. I ached for a shower.

Unfortunately, I learned our plans would have to change a little. With water low on the St. John, there wasn't enough for the plane to land. Instead, we'd get our flight from Eagle Lake, about twenty miles due south of Fort Kent, which itself was about seventeen miles east and downstream of St. Francis where we had expected to board the plane. I was instructed to paddle to the previously agreed landing spot where someone would stop to portage us by vehicle. I was confused a few moments before realizing that this was not the Eagle Lake of Allagash fame, but a long Aroostook County water body from which the Fish River issued, flowing north to its confluence with the St. John in Fort Kent.

The trip hadn't ended and already I began looking back with nostalgia, became sadly reflective. Physically, I was exhausted as I had expected. But I also felt a warm glow of accomplishment and competence, a euphoric energy.

More puzzling and difficult as it was surprising, was the change in my connection with Alice. Regardless of petty arguments and irritations, our relationship seemed to have ripened prematurely, out of season, like a fruit grown in a hothouse. We'd accelerated the normal give-and-take of getting to know one another. I wasn't sure if that was good or bad or where it would lead. About some things, especially outward needs and preferences, it seemed our knowledge of each other had wonderfully deepened, but when it came to more intimate understandings we were navigating unpredictable shallows not unlike our past day of paddling. We experienced a kind of awkward mutual adolescence, our empathies fully formed in some ways, undeveloped in others. At times we seemed able to not only anticipate, but appreciate and even admire the other's actions and feelings. Yet often we appeared uncoordinated and wholly incompatible.

Being together uninterrupted by the exigencies and distractions of normal routines was nice. We were left free to react to each other absent outside support. Without relief from each other's company for a week-and-half, we'd learned to work as a single entity regardless of disagreements and difficulties. But, we were also pulled apart by the same tenacious zeal enabling us to survive adverse circumstances. The trip was dense, our experience of each other compressed beyond normal time limits. Events had the effect of weeks and months. Although the passion of our mutual attraction was invigorating, I found hard feelings easily accumulating with difficult, inescapable centrifugal experience. "A canoe trip," wrote McPhee, "is a society so small and isolated that its frictions—and everything else about it—can magnify to stunning size."

Would the relatively new relationship Alice and I had forged outlive the small triumphs and hardships of our time on the Allagash? How well prepared, I wondered, did it make us for life's more difficult voyages ahead.

Such were my thoughts as I made dinner while Alice rested in the tent. I was stirring a pot of noodles when a dark haired, athletic-looking man of about forty strode into our camp with a swagger of authority. "I'm the cheapest man in town," he announced loudly by way of introduction.

Dressed in lumberman's clothes, he began reciting his services—transportation, canoe rental, fishing guide and the like—without so much as extending his hand, let alone giving his name. He seemed crestfallen when I told him we had no need of his services, yet he continued reciting his offerings. "I live in the big blue house a couple miles upriver. Didn't you see my sign?" I remembered a crudely lettered board, though it failed, like him, to give the rates for various services. Based on the way he looked around, I suspected that costs depended somewhat on his assessment of one's ability to pay based on the appearance of individuals and the quality of their gear. He continued on about his hunting and fishing guiding. Looking for a way to break the conversation, I told him I had to get busy about making dinner. He could, at least, see that was true.

He scribbled his name and number on a piece of paper. "If you recommend someone to me, I'll make it good to you," he said as we shook hands. As he walked away, I wondered how exactly he "would make it good," since he didn't even know my name. Such was our welcome back to civilization. We had not even gotten off the river when someone tried selling us something.

ST. JOHN

We were out of the tent and cooking breakfast before five o'clock. An early start was needed to reach
St. Francis, fifteen miles down the St. John River,
where I'd arranged to meet the truck that would
haul us to our rendezvous with the seaplane on Eagle Lake. Heavy
fog rose into the frigid air from off the water and amplified the
darkness. A hard frost had set overnight and both tent and canoe
were covered with a crunchy veneer of ice. Freshly out of bed and
shivering, our hands reddened and stiffened as we cooked a breakfast of oatmeal and canned sausage while packing the gear. Light
was not fully on the landscape when we put-in at about 6:30, and
what little there was became diffused in the fog.

At it's confluence with the Allagash, the 1830s geological report noted, the St. John "is a broad, deep river, running quick,
often with rapids dangerous to small boats, by their swell, and
is bordered by high banks of sand and gravel." We were glad to
have such a description, for we hardly saw either banks or river in
the dense, swirling fog. Visibility was but a couple yards and we
strained against the gauzy air. Alice was a fuzzy outline at the other
end of the boat, and I shouted constantly to aid her in steering
through the rapids because gestures could not be clearly seen. We

were chilled and wore wool socks on our hands for want of gloves.

Fog blew in breathy patches, revealing and then concealing the countryside. Islands that are said to lie at the confluence remain a mystery to me. Navigation required listening to and watching the water. We could see the flow, but not the river, not the landscape.

We finessed our way through several rapids and over gravel bars with only our ears for guidance, like blind people tapping canes. Rocks loomed suddenly out of the mist, but we heard water running around them first. We became stuck in two places and got out to drag the canoe. Fortunately, we managed to find stepping stones and kept our feet dry. It was a tense, adrenaline-pumping paddle. We didn't know what was coming until we were there.

About a mile below the Allagash, Hubbard described the St. John as a wide expanse with strips of grass-tufted meadow dotted with vase-shaped elms rising toward distant mountains. Cattle grazed along the shore, along with a group of "mouldy" buildings and an occasional ruined mill. Again, I was glad to have a description since the world around us remained barely visible.

At eight o'clock mist was still on the water, although it was lifting in patches, playing hide-and-seek with the countryside. Fog created a variety of shapes from the green hillsides and made guesswork of the shoreline, forging contours in imagination. Eventually, a strong, but not hot sun sponged up the mist and a pastoral valley patched in meadow and forest and stippled with tight little houses was revealed. Stanton found a "wide valley, dotted with little hamlets and productive farms, with ranges of mountains in the background." Seeking only "the wildest country," Thoreau decided not to venture here, fearing "the banks of the St. John were much too settled."

After the endless Allagash woods, we could hardly pay attention to paddling so distracted were we by this gardened landscape. Near the mouth of the St. Francis River, with the bright green hills of Canada in view, we pulled in at Pelletier's picnic ground and put down our paddles. A brightly painted rock marked the seaplane landing.

Despite a dry season with slower current, the St. John had taken us more quickly downriver than anticipated. We spent some time lying on shore out of the wind, soaking up rays brightening the hills and reflecting off the water. After over a week on the move, I was restless. With my body still, my mind began roaming. Reflexively, I pulled my notebook out of its four plastic bags and began writing. Alice looked askance, did a double-take, and then broke into a big gap-toothed grin, which I took as approval, or at least tolerance. My pen seemed suddenly light and dashed rapidly against the damp, dog-eared pages.

What, I wondered, drew people to a place like the Allagash that had neither true wilderness nor, on the other hand, resort conveniences. Even strictly from a paddler's viewpoint it was lacking. It didn't offer the best fishing for rod and reel enthusiasts or a carnival ride of rapids for whitewater types. Yet despite its shortcomings, the Allagash continues to be a dream destination for many in search of a landmark outdoor experience.

In the nineteenth century, a trip to the Maine woods was a panacea. Some saw it as a respite from the rat race, an opportunity to relax and improve digestion and appetite. Others crowed about the benefits of exercise. These remain common reasons for an Allagash journey.

Though his expectations may have been a bit grand, I sympathized with the idealistic Winthrop who thought that one might "see the visible, and hear the musical, and be stirred by the beautiful. These, truly," he wrote, "are not far from the daily life of any seer, listener and perceiver; but there, perhaps, up in the strong wilderness, we might be recreated to a more sensitive vitality." His words are inspiriting, with a power that resonates even a century-and-half later. No doubt it was just such inspiring words and unbridled idealism that enabled Major Winthrop to rally his troops for a final ill-fated charge against Confederate lines at the battle of Big Bethel, Virginia on June 10, 1861. He took a bullet in the chest as he stood on a downed tree trunk, waving his sword and urging his men forward. Ironically, it's said, staunch abolitionist Winthrop was felled by a black slave fighting alongside his master.

Today we seek the backcountry for many of the same reasons, though perhaps without such grand hopes. Thoreau railed against the base motives with which most people went to the woods in his day—for logging, hunting, and cultivating—without any love for the forest itself. Now the balance may have shifted, at least in special places like the Allagash. Most come here as Thoreau did— as students and observers. They use the rhythms of the river and canoe to sort through life, provide a contrast, renew their physical and mental vigor, and increase their appreciation of both civilized and wild places. It is recreation that is re-creation. This is a small river that has grown vast because of the simultaneous call of the loon and presence of locomotives.

Little more than an hour passed when we were greeted by Mr. Pelletier, a loquacious older man with a welcoming smile. He helped load our gear onto his truck for the trip to Eagle Lake. Born in St. Francis, he once lived in Fort Kent for sixteen years. Although he came from a family of schoolteachers, he was entrepreneurial by nature and ran a campground, canoe rental, outdoor gear outfitting and transportation businesses, as well as the local motel. He had owned the store next to his home, but he'd sold it a couple years earlier so he and his wife could travel. Sadly, she'd died from cancer about a year ago. He'd since taken several trips—to the west coast, Egypt, Israel, and soon Hawaii. His wife, he said, would have wanted it that way.

Speaking in a down east accent with slight French inflection, he'd talk rapidly for a sentence or two and then, as if changing gears, slow down and get quieter until suddenly revving up to his original pace and volume. Often such transitions signaled a change of subject, but he'd somehow always circle back to his original thought.

Most people in Allagash and St. Francis, he noted, worked in the timber industry. As you got to Fort Kent there were more farmers. It was mostly potatoes, but with hard times for the tubers, oats were increasingly grown.

In thrall to his voice, I could have listened to Pelletier for days. Though it must have been an hour's ride, it seemed but a moment before he was untying the canoe as we unloaded our gear beside a dock at the edge of a large sheet of water. He had traveled to distant, foreign lands, but he was still rooted to his place. More than that, he was as much an essential element of that place as the bedrock, as the river. He was so closely tied to where he lived, that this small part of the world would be recognizably different without him. What did it take, I wondered, to so naturalize oneself, to in a sense become indigenous?

The pilot strapped our canoe to a pontoon and we stuffed both gear and ourselves into the Cessna's cabin, a space which seemed no bigger than the interior of my Datsun two-door sedan. Off we went with a roar, the plane filling with rattle and hum, shaking and noise. Over a thousand feet below us, the landscape was arrayed like a map. It was rugged with hills and then flattened as we approached the large headwater lakes. Katahdin and surrounding mountains loomed regally powerful in gray-green to the south and then east. The mountain's Knife Edge ridge was a jagged gunmetal blade. A cat's cradle of narrow dirt logging roads extended as far as the eye could see, and dust clouds marked the movement of trucks. The pilot pointed out trails of mud in shallow ponds, shadows of where moose had recently tread.

Water sparkled everywhere, and I grasped the topographic logic of rivers and valleys connecting lake to lake. Patches of clearcut alternated with dark green forest and bright bogs. As the vibrating craft splashed into the placid waters of the Penobscot's West Branch like a belly-flopping loon, a young moose bounded out of the river, passing our parked car as it charged into the woods.

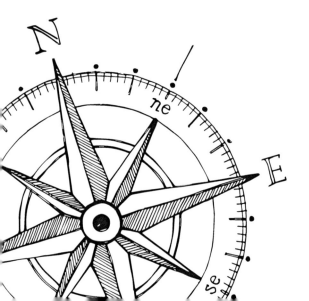

PART III

→

TAKE-OUT

He who hears the rippling of rivers in these degenerate days,
will not utterly despair.
–Henry D. Thoreau, *A Week on the Concord and Merrimack Rivers*

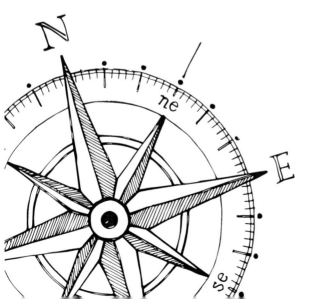

ROMANCE'S DANGEROUS CURRENTS

lice and I left the Allagash triumphant. We had accomplished something as a couple neither of us could have done alone. On returning home, it infused our relationship with renewed energy as we told stories and laughed with friends, the tense trials of the trip transformed into victorious stories of teamwork and endurance. We were rare among people we knew, our relationship having survived grueling labor and the privations of bugs, sleeping on hard ground, adverse weather, primitive hygiene, and a limited and not always tasty diet. We had a special bond, or so we convinced ourselves.

The more we told stories, the more the anger and strained distrust that had erupted on the lakes and rivers faded from recollection. Without fully realizing it, we turned the ten days into an allegory of synergy and coordination, something that presaged success, not just as paddling pals, but as life partners.

At the very least, we were fooled into equating the crucible of canoeing with the pressures and joys of daily life together. It was all too seductive for me. At once I had proved my manhood in conquering the Allagash, lived a Thoreauvian dream of adventure and contact with nature, had a literary topic, and found a mate. A neat package, it seemed to fit almost inevitably and irresistibly well.

"Paddling with a partner," I read a few years later in an essay by
wilderness canoeist Alan Kesselheim, "is very much like dancing."
Having literally spent years of time in a canoe over many trips with
his wife, Marypat, he found that they maneuver "in concert to the
rhythms of current and wave, harmonize . . . interactions, react to
each other's moves, sense in each other's intentions a beat ahead,
read the water notes in the tension of body language." Kesselheim
demonstrated that paddling companions can survive as lovers,
forging bone-deep connections transcending their immediate experience. It takes time, patience and understanding—just like good
dancing. Though Alice and I would try, and even took lessons, we
never learned to dance. I envied Kesselheim.

Alice and I were married a few years after our Allagash adventure. Our honeymoon was a long canoe trip, and we took several
others over the next few years. The fractures that appeared on the
Allagash returned in daily life, but were blurred by our annual
achievements on the water and the tales we later delighted in telling about overcoming hard traveling in the wild. As two strong-
willed people, we made a good team on the lakes and rivers where
we had a common challenge. At home, everything fell apart.

Despite best efforts, the anger, anxiety and frustrations Alice
and I experienced in lightning-like flashes while canoeing, only
grew more profound in our home life. It seemed strange given the
brief but intense amplification of these feelings while on the water,
but the yearly canoe trip seemed a relief valve. Planning, prepara-
tion, the paddling, and ultimate triumph, whether on a voyage to
Alaska or to the edge of polar bear country at Fort Severn, seemed
sufficient distraction, at least temporarily, to quell the tensions and
bigger issues of living together.

After our children were born, long distance canoeing together
ended and life's inevitable tiresome details hungrily devoured our
connection, slowly fraying the bond that had tied us together. Like
many relationships, ours ended in a series of hurts and accusations,

misunderstandings that began seeming intentional affronts. There wasn't a single blow-up, just long days and sleepless nights of drift and discontent that soured the very air, making a mockery of our time on the Allagash.

Ultimately, I felt Alice's very presence devolving into an absence for the understandings and affection I thought we had had, and for what I long hoped we would always have. The empty code words feigning endearment that she flung at me failed by their hollowness and shorted the last electricity of passion. Surrogate reasons for unkind acts appeared like distorted carnival mirrors, and we lived, it seemed, in a land of broken toys. It became the marriage of the "bad attitude." We'd gradually become a tired habit, and eventually succumbed to the inevitable.

At this low point in my life I felt weighted and sluggish, like a canoe too heavily freighted with passengers and gear. I even fell out of sympathy with Thoreau for a while. His once inspiring words seemed like a familiar song played on an instrument hopelessly out of tune.

Soon after becoming Connecticut's deputy commissioner of environmental protection with the job of preserving and managing the state's natural resources along with some responsibility for Indian reservation lands, I began reliving the concerns I had had about Thoreau's attitude toward his Allagash guides. Already in a troubled frame of mind, it was a short leap to thinking that despite hosannas of the modern environmental movement, Thoreau was no eco-saint. In fact, I discovered that he had the opposite reputation in his hometown of Concord after setting over 300 woodland acres on fire in 1844 while cooking his catch of fish in a decaying pine stump. The misdeed was remembered bitterly for years by people blackening their fingers on charred logs they brought inside for cooking and heating.

Although Thoreau was an exponent of unfettered nature and freely roamed the woods without regard to property or political

boundaries, he made much of his living surveying, defining owner-
ships that parceled and made a commodity of his beloved countryside. Even in the woods of Maine, he admitted, "I have a surveyor's
eyes." Far from being a primitivist who shunned all technology as
"but improved means to an unimproved end," Thoreau was adept
at pencil making and developed a number of technical innovations
for the family business. Despair over my marriage bled into, and
seemed to poison my passion for a man whose words and world
had once energized me.

Deeply despondent, my life seemed a sticky tangle of incon-
gruities and loose ends. I took long walks to get away from myself.
Then, one day while sitting in sunshine on a high, mica sparkled
ledge overlooking the Farmington River and the village where I
live, I was suddenly struck by how the contradictions and ambigui-
ties troubling me were not unlike those Thoreau experienced.

Following Thoreau's example, I decided, did not require a life
of ecological perfection. I could still do good work for the Audubon Society even while driving a gas-guzzling pickup truck. A
true Thoreauvian existence first and foremost demanded that I
regularly question my consumptive habits and consider how even
mundane and routine actions can affect the natural world. Furthermore, Thoreau failed spectacularly at romance and never married.
I could salvage a life rich in ecological connections, literature and
friendships, just as he did, even if I stayed single or never paddled
a canoe again.

Once more, I found myself inspired by this man so distant in
time yet seemingly near in every other way. Now, no longer idealizing him as he had his Indian guides, I instead saw his art and philosophy framed in the context of the social pressures and personal
difficulties all of us face. The Thoreau I needed was not the beati-
fied scold and shining exemplar of environmental purity, it was the
man who observed in *Walden*: "Be it life or death we only crave
reality." This reality is messy and rife with hazards, embarrassments
and accommodations.

Long walks in the woods and sitting on windblown hilltops helped heal my relationship with Thoreau, but no amount of trees, birdsong, or fresh air could repair my heart. What was broken would take two willing people to fix. Without a river's challenge or the beauty of the deep forest to mediate the disconnection between me and Alice, I felt adrift, left alone to float with the whim of wind and current.

Someone once told me to concentrate on remembering the good times in wayward relationships. I'd have been better off recalling the bad ones. They're more instructive. Back on the Allagash all those years ago, in thrall to the power and beauty of natural forces, I was dazzled by a kind of high-minded hope that lent our connection an illusory blessing despite sometimes fierce discord compressed between bow and stern. I was late in realizing that the canoe, with all its ambagious means of moving forward in twisting whitewater and fierce unrelenting winds, pointed the correct way like a compass needle. I needed more time before seeing clearly enough to read the obvious and thread a joyous passage through life, find a partner who could teach me how to both give and receive love. That time would come, but not by paddle and portage.

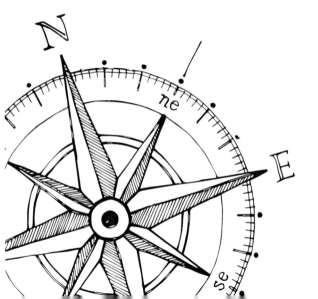

ALLAGASH DREAMS

C alling the Allagash a wilderness is to cling to an ideal, a dream. It's something to reach for, though seemingly always just beyond our grasp. Certainly, it will never meet Webster's requirements of "an area uncultivated and uninhabited by human beings" or an "empty and pathless" region. But the Allagash remains a relatively nearby place where a person can encounter wildness. Abandoned artifacts of past use like the locomotives may actually intensify the sense that people don't belong, are transient. If kept sufficiently distant, perhaps the contrast of continued logging nearby can even highlight wilderness values.

Ultimately, one's sense of wilderness remains deeply personal. Perhaps the fringe of trees along the waterway mimics the beauty strips we create in our own lives, the veneer we present to others. The real exploring is inside this thin, easily bruised curtain. "Be a Columbus to whole new continents and worlds within you," Thoreau wrote near the end of *Walden*. "Every man is an isthmus or inlet, yet unexplored by him" awaiting "the private sea, the Atlantic and Pacific Ocean of one's own being alone."

Chamberlain Lake and Allagash Falls and the waters connecting them are as much an interior topography as a place of rock and water. Here we set a rod and look through a transit for our eyes alone, finding a place that breaks personal routines as we stand in absolute awe of natural grandeur.

We need the Allagash for the rapidly disappearing capacity to find ourselves by becoming lost in nature. The far corners of the globe might be available to those who are hyper intrepid or wealthy or both, but a near-at-hand wild place is a precious asset for the very contradiction of being remote yet accessible. As the planet shrinks with increasing population and speedy travel, such places will only grow in value. We need to protect them. Failure to do so will cause us to face the greatest and most irreversible extinction of all time. Worse than the loss of any animal population or even species, we will have to confront what author Robert Michael Pyle has called the "extinction of experience," a "mass estrangement from things natural."

Regardless of how the woods are managed, historic artifacts are curated, or the number of people that are allowed at campsites, Allagash dreams will persists as long as the big lakes brim with water and the river flows, as long as we have the descriptions of joy and adventure from Thoreau and other writers. There will always be an Allagash of myth and vision, a stream of powerful inspiration.

A single experience on the Allagash can touch us for life, shape our future. Decades have passed, and still I reach back in memory for illumination and strength. It's a place my mind likes to linger. Simply knowing the river is there lends significance to existence, just as it's important for our sense of the world that the Grand Canyon or Machu Picchu exist, regardless of whether we ever visit them. When frustration sends life south, my spirit flows north.

In that respect, not much has changed since my time on the river. On the Allagash, wilderness waterway superintendent Matthew LaRoche wrote in the September 2014 *Northwoods Sporting Journal*, "you will notice that a peaceful feeling starts to take hold of you on about day number two." By the third day, "the rhythm of paddling will have subconsciously taken over your thoughts" and "the constant reading of the watercourse becomes your primary focus." A man who enjoys calling moose, trout fishing, and grilling Spam on a stick over an open fire, he attributes much of that peaceful feeling to "getting away from modern communications technology," devices that didn't exist in 1983. It was LaRoche, then a seasonal ranger, whose smile and tail wagging black Labrador greeted Alice and me back then, hauling our gear around Chase Rapids in his pickup. Clearly, the tranquility and simplicity that Allagash travelers experience in contrast to daily life is even more pronounced today than when I floated those waters.

My Allagash journey started as a kind of pilgrimage toward a variety of goals. Like many others, I was a seeker of Thoreau and the mythic Maine he created. Ultimately, I didn't know what I would find beyond bragging rights at having navigated those legendary lakes and rivers. Perhaps the first thing I learned was a species of Thoreauvian simplicity in the basic routines of primitive travel, the rhythms of strenuous activity, simple food, and regular rest as I tested myself against terrain and weather.

I quickly discovered that a trip such as this was less to be measured in miles than in sharpened perceptions. Travel, it seemed, was worthwhile not just for new sights, sounds and smells, but for the way in which it enlarged experience generally. On my return home, I began looking at nearby people, places, things and phenomena in the heightened, purposeful way I did while on the Allagash. Natural beauty, clues to the past, intriguing characters, and connections between personal experience and the larger world erupted down the street and around the corner. Years later, I found Thoreau contemplating like thoughts not long before his final Maine excursion. "Only that traveling is good," he confided to his journal on March 11, 1856, "which reveals to me the value of home and enables me to enjoy it better."

The Allagash may be a lesson in difficult juxtapositions. The give-and-take and often unholy compromises between man and nature on the waterway are not only instructive for wild rivers and remote wildernesses, but for vacant lots and scarred hillsides in thickly settled areas near home.

"The most alive is the wildest," Thoreau asserted in his essay "Walking." But he primarily experienced this aliveness by wandering widely in his well-peopled and cultivated native town, and headed north to Maine only on occasion. "The poet, must, from time to time," he observed at the end of his first Maine journey, "travel the logger's path and the Indian's trail, to drink at some new and more bracing fountain of the Muses, far in the recesses of the wilderness."

Although I've forgotten details over the decades, the river still exerts a powerful influence in the way I encounter the world. It has cascaded through me all those years, sharpening senses to my surroundings as surely as water tumbles and foams over rocks below Churchill Dam. A deep and abiding correspondence has emerged between me and that landscape, a bond welding the Allagash to my imagination as if it were the bracing fountain Thoreau described.

I found the Allagash profound, not just for elemental encounters with nature, but for the way in which it tested my assumptions about personal relationships. While for the most part I adequately read the river's current and generally found safe passage through whitewater, my reading of personal stream channels was halting and awkward, dangerously misconstrued like a foreign language only partially understood. In retrospect though, the river taught me much in that regard too. Once I developed the capacity to perceive what it had been teaching, I realized that in relationships, like rivers, you respect the current, eddies and wind, sometimes employing indirect, yielding means to go with the flow and get you where you need to be. This perception came too late in my time with Alice, but it would later open worlds of deep and fulfilling intimacy I might never otherwise have discovered.

Despite snickers about a staged wilderness, the Allagash offers real and valuable challenges near to millions. It's a gentle wild place where youth can test their mettle, middle-agers can prove they still have the mojo, and elders can enjoy a last look at true grandeur.

The mythic landscape created by Thoreau and others has proved as valuable and challenging as that wrought of wood, water, and stone. One buttresses the other. And each generation and every individual is free to find their own Allagash regardless that many others have been there.

With its contradictions of accessibility and wildness, rough history of resource extraction and idealized adventure, unique literature, and ongoing tension between nature and civilization, the Allagash is not only a natural force, but a metaphor for human experience. Why else does it dwell so deeply in the hearts of those who have been there?

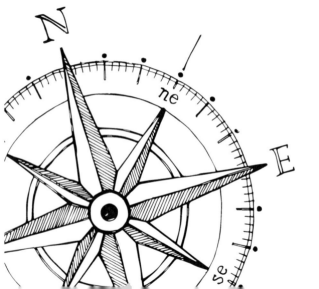

SOURCES

Allagash literature over the course of three centuries is rich and varied. It is a least as deep as the headwater lakes and as long as the river. It ranges from poetic literary treatments in hardbound books to journal-like trip notes found on the internet. There are volumes featuring artistic photos, articles of straight forward reportage, pamphlets, government reports, and exposés and polemics by private groups and individuals. It would be a goodly sized book that provided a reasonably comprehensive bibliography. I offer only my main stem influences.

Scripture on the subject is, of course, Henry David Thoreau's *The Maine Woods*, first published in by Ticknor and Fields of Boston in 1864. The contemporary definitive version, which I use, was published in 1972 by Princeton University Press, and is particularly valuable for its index, historical and textural introductions and other scholarly apparatus. For more of Thoreau on rivers, read his first book, *A Week on the Concord and Merrimack Rivers*, published by James Munroe and Company in 1849, also available from Princeton University Press (1980).

In addition to Thoreau, my nineteenth and early twentieth century companions on the Allagash included Theodore Winthrop, *Life in the Open Air, and Other Papers, Ticknor and Fields* (1863);

Thomas Sedgwick Steele, *Canoe and Camera: A Two Hundred Mile Tour through the Maine Forests*, Orange Judd Company (1880) and *Paddle and Portage, From Moosehead Lake to the Aroostook River, Maine*, Estes and Lauriat (1882); Lucius L. Hubbard, *Woods and Lakes of Maine: A Trip from Moosehead Lake to New Brunswick in a Birch Bark Canoe*, Ticknor and Company (1883) and Hubbard's *Guide to Moosehead Lake and Northern Maine*, 5th ed., published by the author (1893); Fannie Hardy Eckstorm, "Down the West Branch of the Penobscot, August 12-22, 1889," Benton L. Hatch, ed., Appalachia, (December 1949); and G. Smith Stanton, *Where the Sportsman Loves to Linger: A Narrative of the Most Popular Canoe Trips in Maine, The Allagash and East and West Branches of the Penobscot*, J.B. Ogilvie (1905).

Later twentieth century companions included U.S. Supreme Court Justice William O. Douglas whose *My Wilderness: East to Katahdin*, Doubleday and Company, Inc. (1961) includes a chapter entitled "Allagash;" Edward Hoagland whose *Walking the Dead Diamond River*, Random House (1973), includes "Fred King on the Allagash;" John McPhee, *The Survival of the Bark Canoe*, Farrar, Straus, Giroux (1975); J. Parker Huber, *The Wildest Country: A Guide to Thoreau's Maine*, Appalachian Mountain Club (1981, second ed. 2008); and famed Maine guide Gil Gilpatrick, *Allagash: The Story of Maine's Legendary Wilderness Waterway* (1983).

Allagash country living was described by schoolteacher Helen Hamlin in *Nine Mile Bridge: Three Years in the Maine Woods*, W.W. Norton & Company, Inc (1945); and lock tender Dorothy Boone Kidney in *Away From it All*, A. S. Barnes (1969), *Home in the Wilderness: Away From it All in the Allagash Woods of Maine*, Gazelle Book Services, Ltd (1977), and *Wilderness Journal: Life, Living, Contentment in the Allagash Woods of Maine*, G. Gannett Pub. Co. (1980).

Other books with useful historical and descriptive information include Moses Greenleaf, *A Survey of the State of Maine*, Shirley and Hyde (1829, reprinted by the Maine State Museum, 1971); Charles T. Jackson, *First Report on the Geology of the State of Maine*, Smith and Robinson (1837); *The Penobscot Man*, Fanny Hardy Eckstorm, Houghton (1904); Lew Dietz, *The Allagash: The History of a Wilderness River in Maine*, Holt, Rinehart, and Winston (1968); Roioli Schweiker, ed., *AMC River Guide, Volume 1, Maine*, Appalachian Mountain Club (1980); Dean Bennett, *Allagash: Maine's Wild and Scenic River*, Down East Books, (1994); and Don J. Lavoie, *Allagash Origins*, North Country Press, (2013).

Among the maps I used were "Allagash & St. John, Map & Guide," DeLorme Publishing Co. (undated); "Allagash Wilderness Waterway," Bureau of Parks and Recreation, Maine Department of Conservation (undated); and the following U.S. Geological Survey topographic maps: "Allagash," "Allagash Falls," Allagash Lake," "Caucomgomoc Lake," "Chesuncook," "Churchill Lake," "Musquacook Lakes," "Northeast Carry," "Round Pond," "St. Francis," "Telos Lake," and "Umsaskis Lake."

Of course, there was no available internet in 1983 when I paddled the Allagash. Today there is a broad range of information on the web from official government documents to trip reports, photos, analyses by conservation organizations, and advertisements of outfitters. In putting my old manuscript together and constructing the "Put In" and "Take Out" sections, I fact checked and explored using internet resources. I won't reference them here except to recommend the Maine Department of Agriculture, Conservation and Forestry site. It includes descriptive materials, rules, history, fees and lots of other useful information. A lot of the old-time books and articles I tracked down at rare book and other libraries are now available on the net. It's a very convenient shortcut, but I would not trade the awe of paging through an original historical document in the hushed recesses of a library for such ease.

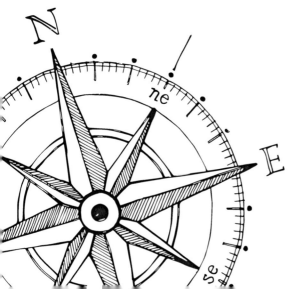

ACKNOWLEDGMENTS

A book such as this does not come into being without a good deal of inspiration and assistance, some intentional and some inadvertent. Most of all I want to thank my wife Mary Fletcher and my friends Amy Nawrocki and Eric Lehman for their encouragement. I also owe a good deal to L.M. Browning, my editor and the founder of Homebound Publications who first saw the possibilities in this long dormant project. Additional kudos go to Eric for wading through an earlier manuscript version of this work and gifting me with invaluable detailed comments. Mary also has a fine ear for language and offered many insightful observations about the narrative. Her suggestions greatly improved the book.

I am grateful to Matthew LaRoche, Superintendent of the Allagash Wilderness Waterway and Cathy Johnson, Northwoods Project Director for the Natural Resources Council of Maine, for their willingness to field my questions on long phone calls. I am indebted to Walter Opuszynski and his colleagues at Northern Forest Canoe Trail for help with maps. I also want to thank all the many librarians who have helped me over the years, especially those at Yale's several libraries including the Beinecke and Sterling. Finally, I once again must reveal my deep indebtedness to Beth Van Ness, Reference and Adult Services Librarian at my hometown

Canton, Connecticut Public Library, for her tireless assistance and good cheer in locating the most obscure document or book and the oddest quote.

Of course, despite the best of assistance and intentions there are bound to be mistakes. They are the author's sole property.

ABOUT THE AUTHOR

David K. Leff is an essayist and poet and former deputy commissioner of the Connecticut Department of Environmental Protection. His work focuses on the surprisingly intimate relationship of people to their built and natural environments. His nonfiction book, *The Last Undiscovered Place* was a Connecticut Book Award finalist. He is the author of three other nonfiction books, *Deep Travel, Hidden in Plain Sight* and *Maple Sugaring: Keeping it Real in New England.* His poetry collections are *The Price of Water, Depth of Field, Tinker's Damn* and *Finding the Last Hungry Heart.* His work has appeared in the *Hartford Courant, The Wayfarer, Appalachia, Yankee, Connecticut Woodlands, Connecticut Coastal, Canoe & Kayak,* and *The Encyclopedia of New England* and elsewhere.

David is a trustee of Great Mountain Forest in Norfolk, Connecticut and on the Collections Steering Committee of the Connecticut Historical Society. He has served on the boards of the Riverwood Poetry Series, Connecticut Forest and Park Association, the Connecticut Maple Syrup Producers Association and Audubon Connecticut. He has taught nature poetry at the famed Sunken Garden Poetry Festival and elsewhere. David has been a contest judge for the Connecticut Poetry Society and given poetry readings at venues throughout the state. He has lectured on environmental and historical topics, the craft of writing, and other subjects on college campuses, at conferences, for annual meetings and at other events. David is the town meeting moderator and town historian in his hometown of Canton, Connecticut where he also served 26 years as a volunteer firefighter and in other civic activities.

WWW.DAVIDKLEFF.COM

HOMEBOUND PUBLICATIONS

Ensuring that the mainstream isn't the only stream.

At Homebound Publications, we publish books written by independent voices for independent minds. Our books focus on a return to simplicity and balance, connection to the earth and each other, and the search for meaning and authenticity. Founded in 2011, Homebound Publications is one of the rising independent publishers in the country. Collectively through our imprints, we publish between fifteen to twenty offerings each year. Our authors have received dozens of awards, including: *Foreword Reviews'* Book of the Year, Nautilus Book Award, Benjamin Franklin Book Awards, and Saltire Literary Awards. Highly-respected among bookstores, readers and authors alike, Homebound Publications has a proven devotion to quality, originality and integrity.

We are a small press with big ideas. As an independent publisher we strive to ensure that the mainstream is not the only stream. It is our intention at Homebound Publications to preserve contemplative storytelling. We publish full-length introspective works of creative non-fiction as well as essay collections, travel writing, poetry, and novels. In all our titles, our intention is to introduce new perspectives that will directly aid humankind in the trials we face at present as a global village.

WWW.HOMEBOUNDPUBLICATIONS.COM

CPSIA information can be obtained at www.ICGtesting.com
Printed in the USA
BVOW01s1656020916

460684BV00002B/7/P

9 781938 846335